THE ELEVENTH
COMMANDMENT

THE ELEVENTH COMMANDMENT

ON THE NATURE OF
THE CHRISTIAN COMMUNITY
OF FAITH

JONATHAN FLETCHER

Denver

ST MAXIMUS
SCRIPTORIUM

Published in the United States by
St. Maximus Scriptorium
14 Inverness Drive East, Suite F-160
Englewood, CO 80112
(303) 708-1632
www.stmaxscript.com

ISBN: 978-0-9838399-2-7

Library of Congress Cataloging-in-Publication Data is available upon request.

Cover Design: Jarrod Joplin

Cover Art: *The Promise,* ©Morgan Weistling, licensed by The Greenwich Workshop, Inc. www.greenwichworkshop.com

Interior Layout: Samizdat Creative

Publisher's Note

The Revised Standard Version (RSV) is used throughout this text unless otherwise noted.

To Father Gregory Caruthers, S.J.
without whose steadfast encouragement and friendship
this effort would be much the poorer.

CONTENTS

PREFACE

When I became a Catholic in 2009, I was thrust into an entirely new culture. Having been a "cradle" Episcopalian all my life, except for brief stints as a Methodist, Baptist (the northern variety), and Wesleyan, I was conditioned by liturgy, hymnody, polity, pageants, bazaars, and the predominant way in which the Episcopal Church approached Christian formation—Sunday school. In the process I developed a certain sensibility regarding the way in which the Church gathered people in—and sometimes ran them off. The connective tissue between people in Episcopal parishes was complex but ever-present. The whole process of being in some form of community has always been a subtle part of my church consciousness. I have taught 6th grade and adult Sunday school classes, both solo and as a collaborative effort with a number of pastors of the churches I attended. It was only after I became a Catholic, however, that I started to see this whole process of community building as of central importance to the way we worship and the way in which we translate that worship into our lives.

The most obvious difference I found between the Protestant and the Catholic cultures was the lack of adult Sunday school in the latter. This discovery started a process of exploration that ultimately resulted in this book. The more I viewed my own situation in the context of the Catholic

Church, the more I started to broaden my interest in how the community of faith had operated in my previous encounters with my Protestant brethren. How is true community nourished? What challenges stand in the way of the community-building process? While each experience looked a bit different, there were a few overarching lessons I observed. Numbers matter—very small churches have a huge advantage over larger churches where community building is concerned. Logistics matter—those with one service on Sunday have a great advantage over those with multiple services, if one is trying to connect folks rather than divide them. Culture matters—those who see the whole Sunday experience as one of community building have an advantage over those who see the worship service as the central spiritual experience and Sunday school as essentially an optional catechetical exercise to be chosen if the particular topic *de jour* is of interest. Families matter—those that have a strong broad-based children's program are at an advantage over those that do not, since parents are more available to participate in community building if their children participate. Space matters—those with the physical space necessary to offer different kinds of meeting places are at an advantage over those that have limited meeting spaces. The challenge, therefore, is to consider carefully what a community of faith could and should look like from an examination of past experience as well as from a consideration of the early Church's way of life.

So, what is to follow is an attempt to crystallize what I have learned through my own journey about the Christian community of faith—what it is, how it works, when it doesn't work and why. Particularly, what are the various aspects that take it from being a group of folks who share something in common and may or may not know each other's names to one in which the spirit of love, truth, and transparency allows the life of God to flourish? Each denomination brings something to the table—some portion of the full understanding of the incredible power of a vital community of faith. The way in which these various pieces of the ecclesiastical puzzle can enhance each other and fill out the total picture is the challenge before us.

This book is divided into four parts. Part I describes my own experiences in a number of Christian communities—how they worked, how they stumbled, and how they showed the immense possibilities that could flow from a deep community of faith. Part II is a more formal look at the sources of our understanding of Christian community, emphasizing what I have called "the eleventh commandment." Part III discusses the dimensions of a mature community of faith. As I mentioned above, all of my understanding of how a true community of faith can and probably should operate has come from my own personal experiences—the churches I have attended, the people I have known, and the situations I have found myself in—both positive and negative. There have been moments of anguish and great joy, moments of frustration and great fulfillment, moments of disgust and moments of great gratification. The wonder of it all is that I truly believe God has been at work in all of it. Part IV looks at a number of different contexts in which the community of faith must operate and the resulting challenges associated with bringing it about. I end with our own modest effort at my current parish as one illustration of how the process of community building can take place.

As I reminisce about my experiences in a number of Christian denominations and congregations, let me assert unequivocally my profound debt to those who tried their best to reflect the teachings of Jesus Christ. In no way do I want to appear overly critical. We all fall short of the glory of God. On the other hand, it is difficult to talk abstractly about a subject that is essentially experiential. That is the whole point. The community of faith is a place of experience, so it only makes sense for me to start from my own experiences. I will try to walk a fine line between exposition and judgment. I will try to talk about what I experienced without being judgmental regarding the ways in which it fell short of some yet-to-be-revealed ideal. This may seem ridiculously hard to do, but I hope you will sense a level of generosity toward all those, including myself, who have tried to be true to the vision of Jesus Christ.

Let me also place an important limitation on the table. I am going to be ranging over a large number of areas of which I am not an authority. It is highly probable that I will make statements with which you will disagree, because your experience contradicts my own. I would simply ask for your forbearance and willingness to look beyond my errors to the bigger picture I am trying to paint.

Before we get started, I should take care of a few housekeeping details. Although there is much merit in capitalizing pronouns that refer to God, Jesus, and the Holy Spirit in order to show our deep and abiding respect and adoration, the original Greek in which the earliest manuscripts of the New Testament were written do not do so. I will follow that convention here. While I try always to be inclusive in my language, sometimes for the sake of grammar and syntax the use of "he" for "he and she" and "man" for "mankind" seemed more appropriate. It was also pointed out to me that many Protestant churches do not refer to their congregations as parishes. Having come from both an Episcopal background

and a current Catholic tradition, I tend to refer to all individual church communities as either parishes or congregations, depending on the context. Please forgive me, but I will
use the words parish and congregation interchangeably. I will
also use a small "c" when referring to local churches and a
capital "C" when referring to the Church in a broader context or as part of the proper name of a specific church body.
In other words, I will talk about *a church* and *the Church.*

The problem associated with designating the worship service is also worth mentioning. As a Catholic, we call our
worship services the mass from the Latin word *missa,* meaning dismissal or "go forth." Unless I am speaking particularly
about the Catholics, I will call the worship service—well, the
worship service. I hope this works for everyone. If we can get
beyond these superficial details, I hope we can get to some
deeper shared realities.

So, here we go. In the end, I hope you will see some possibilities in your own church communities for growing into
a true community of faith that Jesus would recognize as a legitimate fruit of his mission, ministry, and saving grace.

PART I

MY JOURNEY

1

AN INTRODUCTION

I tapped lightly on her door and was welcomed into what was the epicenter of the parish's Christian education programs. Sharron, the Director of Christian Education for St. Mary's Catholic Church in Littleton, Colorado, was cordial and generous as she listened to "the new guy on the block" spell out what he wanted to try. I had been attending the church for all of three months (if that), and I am sure she was wondering where I had come from and why I thought anyone should listen to me at all—but she didn't let on. When I finished telling her something of my background as a Protestant and as a recently-minted Catholic and then laid out my thoughts for a group that would meet after mass to talk about Jesus, she suggested that I write up a proposal that she would then pass on to the pastor, Fr. Alvaro Montero. Feeling some encouragement, I left her office with thoughts rushing through my head about what my proposal would look like and how I would enjoy putting all that I had said into some form of organized document.

This encounter was the culmination of what was then a

sixty-five-year journey through various denominations and a multitude of experiences that told me that church should be more than worship, programs, and maybe even Sunday school. The more I struggled with the feeling of emptiness that I was often left with in my church experiences, the more I came to label what I was looking for and not finding as *community*. I had seen glimmers of many aspects of community in all the churches I had attended, but none seemed deliberately to understand or to be trying to implement the full palette of possibilities. Clearly the deepest form of community that captured what I had been seeking was centered on the vague idea I had of *love*. Somehow love and community were inextricably entwined, but I really had only a crude sketch in my mind of how these two concepts worked together—until I started to contemplate this statement of Jesus:

> A new commandment I give to you, that you love one another even as I have loved you. By this all men will know that you are my disciples, if you have love for one another. (John 13:34–35)

How has this new commandment and this description of Jesus' disciples shown itself in the different churches I had attended—and how might it work itself out in my new parish? As I wrote my proposal, I began to appreciate the scope and depth of what I was addressing. I started to understand—well, I am getting ahead of myself. Let me tell you a small part of my story and something of the experiences I have had that have formed the groundwork for this proposal I was asked to write.

2

THE EPISCOPALIANS — I

I was born an Episcopalian, grew up as an Episcopalian, and went to an Episcopal college. For those of you unfamiliar with this denomination, let me offer some meager insight from my own limited perspective. The Anglicans broke away from the Roman Church in the 1500s as a result of a disagreement between England and Rome over the divorce of Henry VIII. Henry decided that since the Pope would not grant his divorce, he would simply make himself the head of the Catholic Church in England—end of problem. As long as the King was going to make himself the head of the Catholic Church in England, those of Henry's supporters with responsibility for implementing this shift in authority might just as well make a few other minor changes to suit their own particular inclinations. The history of the evolution from the Church *in* England to the Church *of* England is a complex one, but the result was basically a church that was founded on the concept of the *via media*—the middle way between Rome, the seat of Catholicism, and Geneva, the seat of Calvinism. In taking this path, the Church of

England continued to uphold Catholic teachings regarding Jesus Christ, while rejecting other teachings that had to do with such things as the authority of the Pope, purgatory, justification before God, sufficiency of Holy Scripture, marriage of the clergy, and the nature of the sacraments. It is called a Protestant church—but for decidedly different reasons than those of the Lutheran and Presbyterian variety. The Anglicans never originally rebelled against the teachings of the Catholic Church. Henry was a Catholic and was given the title "Defender of the Faith" by the Pope for his faithfulness to the teachings of the Church. The Protestant Reformation that involved Luther and Calvin was fundamentally about practice and doctrine. The changes that took place in the Catholic Church in England at first involved only the authority of the King versus the Pope. Only later was there a significant influence by the Protestant reformers.

In practice, what we are left with is basically a Catholic liturgical structure without the hierarchical control, less emphasis on Mary as the Mother of God (although that may be changing), and a Catholic understanding of Jesus Christ without many of the ancillary doctrinal pieces of the puzzle. Some have called it "Catholic Light," but this term betrays a more fundamental shift. The differences have a profound influence over the community of faith. With less hierarchical control, the interpretation of Scripture can be quite varied, not just *de facto* but also *de jure*. The Catholics might differ "in fact," but "by law" the Church has a tight grip over doctrinal interpretation at the top. In other words, Anglicans have none of the topside control to restrict doctrinal interpretation. The *Book of Common Prayer* is the glue that holds Anglicans together. That of course goes for the American expression of Anglicanism as well—the Episcopal Church.

As a Protestant church, it tends to share some more logistical qualities with the Lutherans, Presbyterians, and Methodists—namely, the practice of Sunday school.

My home church in Aiken, South Carolina was St. Thaddeus Episcopal Church. Because we had Sunday school for all children in the congregation, we children were tied together in two ways: the worship service with minimal contact and the time we spent together after the service in Sunday school. We would gather in a small room with a table in the middle. Mr. Gaffias would go through some lesson having to do with a Bible story, and somewhere in the process would pass out bubble gum cigars. I mainly remember the cigars. They were almost sacramental—an outward and visible sign of our inward and spiritual (such as it was) community of faith. We may have done a little praying, but I don't remember that. We may have played games, but I don't remember that. I just remember those cigars—and the fact that we knew each other's names.

In addition to Sunday school we also had summer Bible school, which amounted to a week of daily activities related to having fun in the context of Jesus. The only activity I recall was the gluing of multicolored beads to a small wooden cross. I guess it kept us busy and taught us that Jesus was important. I'm not sure there were any deep life lessons there except maybe having to do with trying to avoid gluing our fingers together. The only other major recollection—and this is major—is that one of my teachers was the most beautiful woman I had ever seen up to that point in my brief life. I was eight and Ray Davis was probably eighteen—my first heart-pounding love. My heart still speeds up a bit when I think of her. She taught me that women were spectacular and worthy of my considerable attention. Only much later did I connect that attraction to a precious God-given gift.

I went to the parish school, Meade Hall, so I would have to say that my communal experience was enhanced by the fact that I saw many of the same kids on Sunday that I saw during the week. There was no special dispensation from Sunday school if you went to an Episcopal school. I don't recall any specific religious training, so there was never a question that school was a substitute for Sunday school.

When I was in high school we had EYC, Episcopal Young Churchmen. The only thing I remember about that was that I got sideways with one of the members over some jokes he was telling and the next day at school he popped me in the jaw. I think I did not handle the situation very well, but other than my pride, I did not sustain any lasting injuries. Sometimes we learn by doing stupid things. Groups of people or communities are good places for that—both stupid actions and learning. I apologized to him about twenty years later. Reconciliation is always healing if we are carrying around a bit of guilt.

I went to an Episcopal college, the University of the South at Sewanee, Tennessee. We were required (in the old days) to attend thirty-five daily and seven Sunday chapel services per semester. We submitted "chapel slips" each time we attended, and these were tallied at the end of each semester. One could not graduate unless the chapel attendance requirement was satisfied, so inevitably you would see a few poor hapless seniors attending chapel every day to make up for a wayward past in order to graduate. I went to chapel regularly and found it rewarding—I actually liked it. It didn't enhance my sense of community, because we never gathered to talk about Jesus or how any of this church stuff influenced our lives, but we went, and it infused some form of spiritual appreciation, I guess. There was a peace there. I needed some form of respite from the harrowing experience of majoring in chemistry.

After college, I took a break and didn't attend church until I landed in Grand Junction, Colorado. Since no one knew that I had been a reprobate for the last few years, I decided to start afresh and take up my spiritual journey where I had left off in college. I attended a local Episcopal church, but when I discovered that no one was particularly interested in my being there, I started "sleeping in" on Sundays. It wasn't until a friend of mine from Denver, Boots Stockton, called one day and said she would be in Grand Junction for the weekend and wondered if I would like to go with her to her cousin's church that I received my first exposure to the Methodists.

3

THE METHODISTS

When I attended the Redlands United Methodist Church in Grand Junction, Colorado, Boots and I were warmly welcomed, and my connection to the pastor, Bob Toll, gave me a certain "standing" in the community. I soon found, however, that *everyone* who was new to the parish was warmly welcomed. That is just the way they operated. I was enfolded in a relatively small and tight community that offered the chance to connect intimately with each member as well as to engage in a number of learning and sharing opportunities. These included a Sunday school Bible class led by a retired Congregationalist minister and a book reading group called "Literate Laity."

The Methodists arose out of the Church of England in the late 18th century. John Wesley and other students at Oxford felt that the Church needed both reform and a reinvigoration by a return to the Gospel teachings of holiness and service. By reaching out to those either ignored or abandoned by the Church, especially the working classes, through vigorous preaching, the movement gained momentum. The rule or

"method" by which early Methodists ordered their lives began to be at odds with practices of the larger Church of England and tensions increased. When a shortage of Anglican
priests in the American colonies due to the Revolutionary
War (1775–1783) became apparent, Wesley ordained a number of preachers with the power to administer the sacraments
in America. As a result, the irreconcilable differences made a
split inevitable. Shortly after Wesley's death in 1791, the of-
ficial division was complete.

As in most such cases, once separation began and certainly
once it was complete, leaders felt a certain freedom to follow their own theological leanings. This was especially true
of the Methodists. While originally taken to be a deliberate
approach to the personal growth in holiness through scriptural study, regular Holy Communion, and ministry to those
in need within the context of the Anglican tradition, Meth-
odism relatively quickly took on the flavor of two different
Protestant schools of theological thought—that of Armin-
ius and of Calvin. Consequently the modern Methodists are
considered to be an integral part of mainstream Protestantism. As such, their worship spaces are simple, their worship
services are centered on the pastor's substantial sermon, and
their Sunday experience is characterized by the linking of the
worship service and Sunday school.

So, here I am in this little Methodist church, feeling for
the first time in my life a connection to the members of a
community. I knew them and they knew me. I went to my
first Bible study and found the open dialogue both refresh-
ing and uplifting. It never had occurred to me before that
one could actually discuss the meaning of scriptural passages.
I recall that a rather fundamentalist couple visiting our class
was more than a bit horrified to discover that we were not

sure what the answer was to a question raised in class. For them, the Bible was an encyclopedia of answers to every possible question. For us, on the other hand, it was a leaping off place for dialogue.

Then there was "Literate Laity." Now that was a wide open affair. We met once a month to discuss a book that had been chosen by the group. The only book I remember reading was Leslie Weatherhead's *The Christian Agnostic.* I really don't remember any details beyond that it was just one more opportunity to think about and enter into dialogue about our faith. As the title implies, Weatherhead was asserting that there is a certain openness to our journey in Christ that is healthy. Beyond that I don't recall many details from our time of reading and discussing together—except that one evening we started talking about the Virgin birth and someone (I won't say who) said that he really didn't believe in it. I can hear the words of another member as if they were spoken just yesterday, "Fred (not his real name), I can't believe you said that." Well, as I said, it was wide open and—as far as I was concerned at that stage of my embryonic journey—simply glorious. The fact that we could put our own thinking on the table and get honest feedback was of considerable importance to me. It wasn't so much a matter of what we believed as it was that we could talk openly about it. The dialogue was open, trusting, and full of love.

Probably one of the most important things that happened to me during my stay at Redlands Church was when I was approached by one of the senior members of the congregation and asked if I would like to be the liturgist. Now, you have to understand the way the worship service was structured. The liturgist basically ran the service. The pastor rose to give the pastoral prayer and the sermon, which were, as I

THE METHODISTS

mentioned, centerpieces of the whole worship service. It was up to the liturgist to run the rest of it. So here I am, brand new to this little church and being asked if I would like to "read the service." I was dumbfounded. I stuttered, "But I'm not even a Methodist." The gentleman bore in on me—staring me right in the eye—and repeated, "Jonathan, would you like to *read the service*." I was overcome and blurted out the words, "I'd love to."

The take-away here is the willingness of the community to draw me in by encouraging my participation at the highest possible level. I didn't have to work my way up. I didn't have to earn my stripes or accumulate any credentials. The leadership was paying attention to the fact that I was being changed and that this church experience was at the center of that transformation. I was excited to be there, learning a great deal, and somehow projecting that enthusiasm to others. Their ability to discern that I was ready for something more was quite overwhelming. We all need to be aware that the pie needs to be pulled from the oven right when it is done. Too early and the crust is mushy. Too late and the crust is toast. The plum needs to be picked just when it is ripe. Too early or too late and it is basically inedible. The same thing may be true for people on a journey. The direction that one's journey takes can hinge on one person—a person who is paying attention and is willing to reach out in faith and offer an encouraging and guiding hand at just the right time.

I should relate another little, but quite stunning episode. I was in Missoula, Montana on a mission for Union Carbide's Exploration and Resource Development Department for which I worked. At the end of the week I was to return to Grand Junction, but one of the geologists suggested that I stay over the weekend to ski. As a southern boy, I was just

learning to negotiate the snow-covered slopes and was fanati-
cally enthusiastic about any opportunity to practice. That is
why it was almost as much a surprise to me as it was to them
when I said that I would love to, but I needed to be back
in Grand Junction—*for church.* Say what? *I need to be back in
Grand Junction FOR CHURCH?* Now this was something
entirely new to me. I didn't want to miss a possibly life-
changing event on Sunday with my little Methodist church
community. Maybe something might happen of importance.
I couldn't take the chance of missing it. Imagine, the Episcopal boy become Methodist can't stand the thought of missing
church. You see, real community is compelling and not only
requires commitment, but *entices* it.

Finally, I decided that I should become a full-blown
Methodist, so I sat in Bob's office as he went through the
three-ring binder on the history and nature of the Methodist Church. I don't recall how many meetings we had, but I
think it was just a few. Then at the end of one Sunday service, I was received into the church in a lovely ceremony in
which we held hands and sang a song with the words, "If you
knew the Lord of Heaven was on your side, could you go in
peace? And though we must part, if you were sure he would
abide, would you go in peace?" By this act of mutual reception I became a Methodist. I, with eyes tearing, was greatly moved by the overwhelming generosity of the moment.
While all this may seem a bit mushy to some, remember I am
on a journey, and these folks showed me the love of Christ in
a big and bold way.

But as the old saying goes, "All good things must come to
an end." Bob Toll left Grand Junction for a larger church in
Golden, Colorado, and I found myself in a bit of a dead end
as manager of financial analysis in our Union Carbide office.

I had received a call from Charlie Johnson, the minerals advisor to the Minister of Natural Resources of Botswana, asking me if I would be interested in a similar position in Tanzania. My friend Milt Derrick was leaving Carbide for law school, so all of a sudden the way was clear to "move on." Since I still needed to complete my doctoral dissertation in Mineral Economics at Penn State, I made up my mind that the best thing to do was pursue the potential offer in Tanzania and head back east, leaving the precious Methodists of Grand Junction behind.

When I got back to State College, Pennsylvania, I cast about looking for a church. I went to the Unitarian church in town and found a little too much politics and not quite enough spirituality. (Remember this is all a journey of evolving perceptions.) I didn't even try the local Episcopal church. Maybe I had temporarily given up on them. One day, I was talking to my dissertation advisor, John Tilton, about churches, and he suggested that I go with him to his church. I innocently asked him the name of his church, to which he responded, "The University Baptist and Brethren Church."

I tried not to flinch. *BAPTIST? You have to be kidding,* I thought to myself. Remember, I am a southern boy, and Baptist means *Southern Baptist*—not that I really knew anything at all useful about the Southern Baptists, let alone the northern branch, but I thought I did, and that did not seem to be the direction I wanted to move in. BUT, I liked John and thought he would not be involved in anything "untoward" (whatever that might mean), so I agreed to go.

4

THE BAPTISTS

When I attended the University Baptist and Brethren Church in State College, Pennsylvania, again I was drawn into a relatively small community, all the members of which knew each other well and visibly cared about each other. I happened to have bought my house from one of the "elder statesman" of the church, so I was immediately known as "the person who bought Walter Simon's house"—a status that served me well in my efforts to integrate into the life of the community. The pastor, Mike Scroggins, was a dynamic, warm, and generous force in the church—and a great preacher. I was immediately attracted to the open, generous, and thoughtful embrace of the Baptists.

Northern Baptists—or those belonging to the American Baptist Convention—take their culture and theology from the long and complex history of Baptists in general. As you might suspect, the distinction of being Baptist has something to do with baptism. In fact, it was the rejection of infant baptism and the assertion of the need for the baptized to be competent professing believers that was the foundation of the movement, which can be traced back to the Church of England separatists in Amsterdam in the early 1600s. From there we get a complex mixing of influences including those of the Anabaptists (Dutch Mennonites), whom you would like to think were direct predecessors of the modern Baptists, but which have entirely different roots. Anyway, it is not a simple story. The bottom line is that modern Baptists in the United States find their roots in the First Baptist Church established by Roger Williams in Providence, Rhode Island in 1638. The major split between the northern branch of the family and the southern branch took place in 1845 over the issue of—you guessed it—slavery. The modern distinctions between the two branches are much more interesting and complex than the basis for the historical division might imply. The northern branch tends (and let me stress the term "tends," because there are wide ranging expressions in both branches that allow for much overlap) to be more liberal. The Northern Baptist Convention, to which my little church in State College belonged, was founded in 1907 and changed its name to the American Baptist Convention in 1950. It is interesting that the formation of the convention was an effort to bring more consistency among those churches that identified themselves as "northern Baptists." While the differences between American Baptists and Southern Baptists often can be characterized as those arising from a more liberal or conservative viewpoint, there are still fundamentals that apply to both denominations. Here are a few key aspects of the Baptist faith: (1) believer baptism by immersion—no sprinkling here, (2) soul competency—free will to choose to sin or not, (3) salvation through faith alone—no sense of "works righteousness" or earning your way into heaven by good works or big fat donations, (4) sola scriptura—scripture alone is the basis for faith and practice and as such contains all the knowledge needed for salvation, (5) the priesthood of all believers—there was the pastor, the deacons, and the rest of us—and we all had "standing", and (6) the autonomy of the local congregation—known as a "congregational polity" as opposed to a hierarchical polity as is seen in the Roman Catholic Church. All of these aspects of the church influence the way the community functions at the congregational level.

My particular expression—the University Baptist and Brethren Church—was a joint congregation between the Northern Baptists and the Church of the Brethren. The only thing I ever learned about the latter, even though I was on the rolls of both, was that the Church of the Brethren were very practical Christians who had started the "heifer project," which was grounded on the assumption that missionary work needed to be founded first on satisfying basic needs of hunger before it could address deeper spiritual needs. As a typical Baptist church, our worship was simple, unadorned by liturgy, centered on the pastoral sermon, and spiced by lively hymnody. Mike Scroggins was a master preacher. I think I can still recall many of the sermons he gave, because each was tied to a personal story that gave great light to the theme he was addressing.

One of the interesting and fruitful habits he practiced was to have a "talk back" after every sermon that might be considered controversial. One such sermon involved the assertion that Jesus was a pacifist. Within the context of the post-Vietnam War era (this was around 1980) many would have taken issue with the implications of what he was saying. We would place chairs in a large circle down in the meeting room below the sanctuary (the concept of the priesthood of all believers implied that the sanctuary, where only priests could go, was expanded to include the whole gathering place of the believers). We could then freely challenge him on any of his ideas that we thought were in error or inconsistent with the Gospel as we personally understood it—and he could challenge us right back. One might go so far as to say that he saw himself as both leader and participant in the community of faith. One might also say that everyone in the church saw themselves both as leaders and participants in the life of the community. This process of opening up our search for the truth to the congregation seemed to be a fundamental aspect of true community. As a result, the concepts of shared leadership and participation and a shared search for the truth have become foundational to my understanding of an authentic community of faith.

Of course we had adult Sunday school, although again I am hard pressed to remember details. All I knew was that Baptists would sooner miss the worship service than miss Sunday school, although I am sure this was different in this particular church community, because the sermons were an event not to be missed casually. As a new member, I was immediately drawn into the life of the community, and the intellectual stimulation of learning, questioning, and growing was a critical element of this episode of my journey. I suppose I should relate the story of how I happened to spend one semester in seminary, because it certainly flowed out of my experiences in this congregation as well as the Redlands United Methodist congregation in Grand Junction.

It was a very cold day in February when I walked home from my office in the Mineral Economics Department at Penn State to my little Tudor house on East Prospect Avenue that I had bought from Walter Simons. I had been heating the house that winter with one centrally located wood stove, so I spent a considerable amount of time splitting wood and stoking the fire. After I had managed to heat up the living room, I sat in my grandmother's rocking chair and began to think about my future. Bill Vogely, the remarkable head of the Mineral Economics department, had been putting pressure on me to finish my dissertation and move on to a tenure-track position of assistant professor in the department. It was time to fish or cut bait. As I sat there, I gave myself permission to think broadly about what I really wanted to do—right now. My conclusion was that I should consider selling the house and my used Mercedes Benz 450SLC, putting most of my stuff into storage, loading up my brown International Harvester Scout and heading west—on Route 66 (complete with theme music from the TV show and an air of adventure on the open road).

As I closed my eyes, I imagined myself traveling west through Oklahoma or some similarly semi-flat prairie, when I decided to turn right up a farm road. When I reached the barnyard, the farmer came over and greeted me. I asked what he was doing. He said he was harvesting (I never asked what), at which point I enquired whether he needed any help. He said he did and asked, "What do you need to get paid?" Ah, what did I need to get paid? That one little question was the trigger. I began to reflect on the whole issue of getting paid to do something—and the truth of the moment came crashing in. Some would call it a catharsis or a revelation.

It became abundantly clear to me that the real issue was not what I needed to get paid, but what I wanted to do with my life. The central issue for me at that point was the degree to which I could *give what I had to give*. This realization led to the conclusion that what I *really* wanted to do was to think about God—to study and learn. What I *really* wanted to do was to go to seminary. Tears began to run down my face. I remember going to bed that night and burying my head in my pillow sobbing. Oddly, there was this huge sense of relief. I no longer had to struggle with how I was going to be a university professor in mineral economics. I was going to seek God—the best way I could.

The next morning I went in to see Mike, and I recall him saying as he sat back in his chair with this big grin on his face, "Well, well, I'm not surprised." I don't know why in the world *he* was not surprised—*I* certainly was. He pulled out a brochure on a conference being held that spring at his alma mater, Andover Newton Theological Seminary, in Newton, Massachusetts. He suggested that I go to this or some similar conference to help me sort out the direction I wanted to take. I decided to go to Andover Newton and proceeded to register.

Now I have to tell you this curious little subplot. When I got the schedule, I noticed that it said "Breakfast—Sturtevant Hall, Lunch—Sturtevant Hall, Dinner—Sturtevant Hall." *Hmmm,* my middle name is Sturtevant, so I called my Great Aunt Constance and asked her if there was any reason for there to be a connection between my great-great-grandfather Benjamin Franklin Sturtevant—an inventor and the founder of the B. F. Sturtevant Company[1]—and a Baptist seminary in

---

1 Before WWII the company was one of the largest commercial ventilation companies in the world. Their headquarters was in Jamaica Plain, Massachusetts, south of Boston, and they installed huge ventilation systems in places like the Holland Tunnel (1927), the Lincoln Tunnel (1937), and the tunnels along the Pennsylvania Turnpike (1940). My Aunt Connie told a story of B. F. taking his daughter, my great-grandmother Ella, to the US Capital to view a demonstration of the new ventilation system the company had installed. The story goes that someone threw a cat down the ventilation pipe and it was immediately blown back out. Everyone was duly impressed.

Newton, Massachusetts. She said, "Well, your great-great-grandfather was a staunch Baptist." Huh? A staunch Baptist? I grew up an Episcopalian, and I just assumed that everyone in my family was among the "washed" upper-crust Episcopalians (although there certainly was not anything particularly "upper-crust" about us). When I got to Andover Newton, I asked the director of admissions for whom Sturtevant Hall was named, and he said it was named after—you guessed it—Benjamin Franklin Sturtevant.

Needless to say, I had a wonderful weekend, met a host of warm and generous folks, and had one very moving experience. Toward the end of the conference all the participants were sitting around the outer wall of this large room having been asked to pray about something of personal concern to each of us. When it became my turn, I prayed that our congregation in State College could be healed because Mike, our pastor, had decided to leave and take a call at the First Baptist Church of Worchester, Massachusetts. We all continued to offer our own prayers, and I was rather serenely taking in the moment, when I was roused out of my reverie. A person across the room was thanking God for sending his church, which was broken and deeply hurting, *Mike Scroggins!* Our pain at losing him was somehow relieving their pain by their receiving him. Mike became our gift to them. When I returned to State College, the question arose in the worship service whether anyone had anything they wanted or needed to report (as Baptists are wont to do). I found myself standing and relating my story. It became a healing moment for all of us. We saw our pain in a much larger perspective as the relief of someone else's.

The ASPCA would have cringed, but my understanding was that the cat was fine.

So, what is the point of these stories? My community in State College was a place to grow, to learn, and to share. The love I felt there so permeated my very being that it drove me toward a vocation change, the specifics of which were only vaguely clear to me at the time. I had little idea what I was going to do, except that I was going to seek God and let the rest take care of itself. If a community of faith can do that, there must be something there to explore and to try to replicate.

Although I had a wonderful experience at Andover Newton, and the director of admissions even suggested that they should give me a scholarship (I guess to pay back my great-great-grandfather for his generous gift of the old white clapboard icon at the center of a modern brick campus), I decided to go on a field trip to check out Harvard and Yale. I was sure that a PhD in Mineral Economics would make a very interesting student for them, so I didn't plan my itinerary around selling myself. This approach turned out to be a poor idea. I applied to Yale and was promptly turned down. How could they refuse? I was consequently faced with a big question: Now what? I decided to visit with the founder and director of the Materials Research Lab at Penn State, Rustum Roy, who I knew through our mutual geochemistry connections. I thought, because he was very active in a number of religious organizations, he might have some ideas. His immediate response to my story was, "You don't want to go to *Yale*. They're way too conservative. You want to go to *Union*. I know the president—I'll give him a call."

Well, I really had little idea what the basic differences were between conservative and liberal Christians, so I decided to pursue his suggestion. I dredged up all the possible connections I might have to Union including connections with Penn State professors who knew Union professors and especially the connection between a Union professor and— uh, *my mother.* Robert Seaver taught Mom at a religious drama workshop at Camp Kanuga in Henderson, North Carolina. In other words, this time I was pulling out all the stops and planning my trip to Union around *contacts.* One stunning thing happened when I sat down to chat with Mr. Seaver. I told him some of my story and the fact that my mother had taken a workshop with him at Kanuga about thirty years before. He brightened up and said quizzically, "Gert Fletcher?" I couldn't believe that he actually remembered her. I took that to be a sign. I would apply to Union.

Well, it turned out that my multipronged attack had won the day. I got a call from the Academic Dean on August 10, 1981 notifying me that I had been accepted. I sold my house, sold my old Mercedes Benz 450 SLC, put piles of stuff into storage, filled up a U-Haul trailer and my Scout, and headed off to New York City.

5

UNION

While Union Theological Seminary was not exactly a different denomination, it might as well have been. It has Presbyterian roots as expressed by the presence of Auburn Seminary, a resident administrative office for Presbyterian students at Union (at least that is how it seemed to function when I was there). Union was founded by the Presbyterian Church in 1836 and removed itself from denominational oversight in 1893 over a flap concerning a sermon preached by Charles Briggs that questioned the literal interpretation of Scripture. Auburn Seminary moved to the Campus in 1936. Union was then considered to be one of the major theological universities in the United States, along with Chicago, Harvard, and Yale. Over the years, Union has had many influential faculty, such as Paul Tillich and Reinhold Niebuhr. In addition, Union was and is considered by many to be the center of liberal Christianity in America. It is interdenominational in its orientation and espouses a sweeping openness to all cultures and beliefs. There was a black caucus, a gay caucus, and a women's caucus when I was there. Everyone seemed to be fighting some kind of oppression. James Cone, considered to be the father of black liberation theology, taught me Systematic Theology, and I always wanted to ask him if he loved *whitey*—that would be *me*. I am sure the answer would have been yes, but the rhetoric often seemed to obscure the fact. Roger Shinn taught me Ethics. I recall once writing a paper on the ethical issues associated with Amax (American Metal Climax mining company) mining a mountain near Crested Butte, Colorado for molybdenum. The problem for the locals and Sierra Clubbers was that the beautiful mountain would eventually be mined away. No more beautiful mountain. Nadda! Nulla! Niente! Because of my industrial experience, I took a position that the market and government regulations should be sufficient to address any ethical issues and relieve any individuals in Amax of ethical dilemmas. In my interview with Roger, he was very generous concerning my paper, but then proceeded to ask me questions. All I can remember is that my responses were something like, "Well, yes, of course *that* would be true." After three or four questions he had managed to turn my thinking around 180 degrees. This is not a commentary on industrial ethics as much as it is a commentary on a marvelous teacher. Roger Shinn was a precious gem.

I took Old Testament from Phyllis Trible and Church History from Dick Norris, both well known in their respective fields. While I cannot say that I learned much of the scope of theological studies offered—the theological answers—I can at least suggest that I learned something of the theological questions—who is God, who was Jesus, how do theologians formulate questions about these subjects? I came to Union to learn and think about God. I did manage to do that and was exposed to theological resources that would continue to be important in my ongoing growth.

I lived in Van Dusen Hall and got to know many folks who lived near me, especially Bill Jeffries. He was a Methodist who had once been an Episcopalian, so we had something in common—even though I'm not sure what I was at that point. He and I decided that we needed some form of daily prayer, so we would truck down to the small chapel in the building every weekday morning and read the service of Morning Prayer from our own personal copies of the Episcopal *Book of Common Prayer.* In addition to this prayer discipline, I started to think about other aspects of my life at Union. I had been attending St. James Episcopal Church on Madison Avenue (probably the wealthiest church in the world on a per capita basis, but full of very kind and generous folks), so I made an appointment with Hayes Rockwell, the rector,[2] to talk about my experiences at Union and what I perceived to be some spiritual needs I had identified. At some point he noted, "You think you might need a spiritual director?" I coughed inwardly at the thought and then realized that he was right. I just had not thought about it in those terms before. At another point in our conversation he suggested, "You think you might need to make your confession?" Again, I thought I was going to faint until I realized that that was precisely what I had been feeling. In other words, my experience at Union was opening up all sorts of new spiritual avenues for me—whether I wanted them opened up or not.

One experience at St. James Episcopal Church is worth recalling. On my first Sunday there, the usher kindly escorted me down to one of the pews close to the front of the church and gestured to me that this gapingly empty pew

2 This is Episcopal/Anglican speak for the pastor.

might serve me well. I smiled, thanked him, and said that actually I would prefer to sit next to the lady in the pew just behind. I introduced myself and she responded that she was Helen Hennessey. She said that she had not been to church much recently because her eyes were failing, but that she wanted to attend this service, because it was the last time she would get to see her favorite assistant rector, who was leaving. When it came time to go up for communion, I asked her if she would go up. She said that she would if she had some help, at which point I said, "Let's go, you can hold onto me." Helen was eighty-two and I was thirty-five, but we sort of fell in love—in a sort of sweet, innocent way. From then on, every Sunday I would go over to her huge Park Avenue apartment and walk with her to church. She would hang on to me for communion and after church I would walk her home, often spending some time in her kitchen with a cup of tea talking about her life as the widow of a well-known New York gynecologist and my life as a searching student at Union. She passed away a few years after I left New York, but I will always recall with great warmth the precious love we shared for a brief period.

One final recollection I should offer. Before James Cone's class one day, I was talking with one of my fellow students whom I had gotten to know. I asked him if he would like to come over to my apartment for lunch after class. We were talking about all the caucuses and the idea that many folks seemed to be grappling with a wide range of issues. Out of the blue, Ken casually mentioned, "Well, you know that I am gay." For some reason, I was not the least bit phased. This was my friend, and we proceeded to talk openly about our respective personal challenges and struggles. I bring up this discussion not to say something about homosexuality, but about friendship—and how it can pave the way for a true expression of the love of Christ. It is amazing what you can talk about if you trust one another.

In general, these were beautiful people, both students and faculty. It was a wonderful learning experience, and I am indebted to them for that, but after one semester I received my PhD diploma in the mail from Penn State, and this huge weight was lifted off my shoulders. I had been in school for the better part of thirty years, and I had had enough. I decided that if I were going to learn more about God, I would have to do it on my own. So I said goodbye to Union and headed back to Colorado.

It was there that I returned to my Episcopal roots.

6

THE EPISCOPALIANS — II

When I returned to Colorado, I decided to live in downtown Denver—the Belmont-Buckingham apartments, to be exact. Consequently, the most logical place for me to worship was St. John's Episcopal Cathedral a few blocks away. Equipped with my newly-minted PhD in Mineral Economics from Penn State, I was planning to find employment in either the mining or petroleum industry, in which there was considerable activity in Denver at the time. My first effort was to make an appointment with the Dean of the Cathedral,[3] Don McPhail, to see if he could connect me with anyone he knew who might be able to help. This turned out to be one of the more fateful moves that I was to make during my four years in Denver—my work with HBB, Inc.

HBB was an oil and gas exploration company that specialized in putting together exploration "deals" and selling

---

[3] For those of you who may be unfamiliar with the structure, the cathedral is the seat of the bishop, but the dean actually is the functional pastor of that particular congregation.

participation to larger companies with the financial resources to drill wells and operate producing properties. This company was unquestionably the most interesting business enterprise I have ever worked for. After we chatted for a while, Dean McPhail introduced me to an Episcopal priest, Dan Treece, as he was finishing a Holy Communion service at the Cathedral. Dan was very cordial and agreed to meet with me the next day to help me find gainful employment in the oil and gas business. It turned out that he was the petroleum landman at HBB—the person responsible for securing all the land rights necessary to "tie up" a prospect before trying to interest other parties in participating. He also was a key player in "cutting the deals" with prospective participants. That meeting led to an introduction to Joel Mize who ultimately was brought into HBB as a pipeline engineer. Joel brought me with him, and that is how I ended up working at HBB.

Once there, I worked with Joel on a number of projects including an early effort at developing what is known as Coalbed Methane—natural gas that has become trapped within certain kinds of coal beds. I spent much of my time crunching numbers with an early version of Lotus—an electronic spreadsheet program that was preceded by VisiCalc and followed by Excel. Because HBB was a very small company, I got to know everyone there including the President, Don Henderson, and one of the other landmen, Neil Walden. In fact, HBB functioned often as a small community of faith. *Huh?* Well, because we were all practicing Episcopalians, and Dan was an Episcopal priest switch-hitting as a landman, it was a very unusual place. Don Henderson was deeply spiritual and eventually went to seminary to become a priest himself. I remember vividly during Lent watching Dan talking shop on the phone with his Lucchese dress boots propped up on the desk. "Charlie, we can back you in for a third for a quarter[4] if you drill the first well," and then seamlessly gathering with us in the conference room and speaking the words of consecration over the bread and wine for an intimate service of Holy Communion, "For in the night in which he was betrayed, he took bread; and when he had given thanks, he brake it, and gave it to his disciples, saying, 'Take, eat, this is my Body, which is given for you. Do this in remembrance of me.'"[5] All this was an integral part of *work*. In retrospect, it seems almost surreal—this union of business and spirituality—a community of faith at *work*. Dan passed away many years ago, but Don and Neil have remained steadfast friends after the thirty or so years since we worked and prayed together. A greater gift could not have been given than this precious experience.

I also met some wonderful folks at St. John's, including the associate pastor, who is the current Bishop of the Episcopal Diocese of Colorado, Rob O'Neal. I recall taking a Bible course and teaching sixth-grade Sunday school. I also approached the then bishop Bill Frey about the possibility of becoming a lay preacher and was turned down ostensibly for the lack of need at the Cathedral. My disappointment, while not monumental, has to some extent conditioned my understanding of the role of various ministries in the community of faith. We often think that "need" drives ministry. We have ministries to serve needs of the community, the parish, and individuals "in need." As a community of faith, however, we

4 For those of you not versed in the arcane language of the oil patch, "a third for a quarter" means that you get 25% of the project if you pay 30%. It is called "backing in" and is weighted such that the new participant must pay a little more to get into an ongoing project—or at least one that looks like it will be a viable project.
5 They can be found in the BCP on pages 334–335.

also must consider that ministries are places where disciples are formed. Our development as Christians depends on opportunities to minister. The community of faith should be the place where talents and desires are nurtured—where we learn to give our gifts and receive the gifts of others. Perhaps, the perceived "need" is only half of the equation.

Recall the response of the folks at Redlands United Methodist Church who encouraged me to participate—not out of need, but out of a recognition that I was ready to grow. The difference between the response of the bishop and that of the congregation in Grand Junction was that one was more concerned about fulfilling a need and the other was more concerned about nurturing a disciple. I am not criticizing anyone here. We often get caught up in filling needs and when those needs are, after an exhausting effort, finally met, we think we can relax. We have done our job. We have finally filled out the roster, gotten enough folks to be lay readers, satisfied our need for greeters, or gotten enough folks to bring chicken to the pot-luck dinner. When someone else shows up who wants to participate in that area, it is most natural to make a sigh of relief and say, "Thank you, but we have no need right now." Maybe we should periodically be reminded that one of our jobs is not just to satisfy functional needs, but also to help people participate. In some cases, we just might encourage some participants to move on to other ministries so that both they and new participants are able to grow. "But Fred always reads the part of Peter. He would be crushed if he were not asked to do that again." When we hear these kinds of words, we should pay attention to the possibility that we have some growing to do in our understanding of what a true community of faith is all about. All of us should be in the process of *working ourselves out of a job* so that others might grow by *working themselves into that same job.*

I lived and worked in Denver for four years until the oil business tanked in 1985, at which time I returned to Columbia, South Carolina. My mother was still living and it was an opportunity for me to be closer to home and teach earth science at a historically African American college. When I was looking for a church, I eventually talked to a secretary at an Episcopal church close to where I was living. She said most enthusiastically, "Oh no, I don't go here; I go to St. John's in Shandon (a neighborhood near downtown Columbia)." Then and there I decided to visit St. John's.

The first Sunday, I met Rhett Hardy, a lovely lady who took me under her wing and clearly showed me the face of Christ.[6] The rector's sermon that Sunday was about the warm reception he had received at another Episcopal church while he was on vacation. In other words, it was all about community and sharing the love of Christ with others. I was sold. For the next twenty-five years, with the exception of a hiatus as a Wesleyan (see below), I attended St. John's through three rectors and several assistant rectors.

So where should I start to tell of my experience of the community of faith at St. John's? First of all, let me say that I saw Rhett just about every Sunday after my first visit there.

---

6 I have to say something about southern names. One interesting custom is to use last names as first names. You remember Rhett Butler in *Gone with the Wind*? Rhett is a very old and respected family name in South Carolina. My mother was on the radio with Alicia Rhett in Charleston when Mom was teaching at Ashley Hall. Alicia played Ashley Wilkes' sister in the movie version of *Gone with the Wind*. After I had been at St. John's for a while, Henrietta Singletary, who had a son whose first name was Fletcher, remarked quizzically upon learning my name, "Fletcher, that's interesting as a last name." I thought to myself, "My dear Henrietta, Fletcher was a last name long before it was a first name." I do love the South.

This was of critical importance. She was a constant. Someone whose presence I could rely on. This need for consistency in the community of faith is fundamental. If you never see the same people twice, how are you to learn anyone's name, let alone become a member of their spiritual family? Consistency is vitally important in developing a viable community of any kind. Second, we had Sunday school for adults every Sunday, so there was an opportunity to share more intimately our faith journey and engage each other in a variety of learning contexts. There were usually a number of class offerings, so one could choose a class that met a need or served an interest. In general, these gatherings were primarily seen as learning experiences, but they almost always included substantial opportunities to enter into meaningful dialogue—with some limits.

One such opportunity arose when we had a whole series of Sunday school classes on the *Windsor Report*. The American branch of the Anglican Communion, the Episcopal Church (officially known as the Protestant Episcopal Church in the United States of America), had a bit of a falling out with the rest of the Anglican Communion (those that follow the rites and traditions of the Church of England and are in communion with the Archbishop of Canterbury) over the ordination of an openly gay bishop.[7] The result of that

---

7 I must say that the bishop, Gene Robinson, was one of my very best friends in college. I don't know whether he considered me one of his, but from my point of view, he was a marvelous friend. We were in the same fraternity, he was my partner in chemistry lab, we double-dated on a party weekend, and he stayed up all night typing a term paper for me as I wrote it. Greater love hath no man than to stay up all night typing for his fraternity brother. I can see why the Episcopal Diocese of New Hampshire could look only at his immense generosity and capacity to love in choosing him as their bishop.

brouhaha was a request by the Archbishop for the Episcopal Church to justify its actions. This response was entitled the *Windsor Report*. I say all this to let you know that it was a touchy issue, with many Episcopalians taking diametrically opposed "stands"—with opposing factions squaring off with closed minds and hardened hearts. The class began with the handing out of a sheet of paper with the *rules of engagement*. These rules were basically intended to keep tempers from flaring, but sadly had the effect of stifling any real dialogue. The series consisted of a set of presentations on different aspects of the report with a two-session wrap-up at the end led by a retired Episcopal bishop who was attending St. John's as a parishioner. The idea was that Bishop Charles Duval could certainly keep order if things started to get out of hand. He began the first session of the wrap-up by praising all of us for tackling such a contentious issue and being willing to argue peacefully. I raised my hand and gingerly suggested to the good bishop that we really hadn't argued about anything— yet. He thoughtfully said that we would have some time for real dialogue during the last session. I say all this just to point out one almost universal characteristic of church communities—the reluctance to fight. I am not talking about little innocuous disagreements that end in a vote. I am talking about rabid knockdown, drag-out fights in which everyone sees that they have a large personal stake in the outcome. One of the things I take away from my experience with the *Windsor Report* (and the way in which we try to inhibit conflagrations) is the need for the true community of faith to be a place where we can fight. If you look at a variety of healthy relationships, whether they are marriages, enduring friendships, or whole families, one commonality arises—everyone knows how to fight well. It is not that they never fight—it is that when they do, they fight fairly and take the search for the truth as the ultimate goal. I will say much more about this later.

While I was at St. John's, I was involved in a number of committees and responsibilities. Let me say first that it is impossible to be an active member of a parish and not have a host of communal experiences that—either explicitly or implicitly—reflect on the nature of the specific community of faith or on the nature of the concept of community in general. The stories I relate here are not in the least intended to point any fingers. They are just my own personal experiences that have informed my understanding.

As a member of the Christian Education Committee, I met once a month with our Christian Education Director, Faxie Watt, and others interested in both adult and youth Christian formation. It gave me access to the planning and execution of a variety of classes for adults, and more particularly, an opportunity to think about their intellectual and experiential needs. I was fortunate to be able to teach a course on compassion with the rector, Alan Avery. I recall sitting in his garden talking about the class and planning our lessons. It was a delightful experience and showed me the extreme value of the pastor participating intimately in the teaching/ learning process. As I developed my own thinking about the challenge of adult Christian education, one thing that became clear to me was our need for a clearer picture of who Jesus was when he was in his earthly mission. The result of this thinking eventually was a course I taught called *Scratching the Surface of Christian Transformation*—but I am getting ahead of myself. More on this later.

One of the most important things that happened to me during my stay at St. John's was the formation of a little group eventually called the *Tuesday Morning Breakfast Club that Meets on Monday Morning*. It grew out of a book group discussion of Scott Peck's book entitled *The Different Drum: Community Making and Peace*.[8] In it he talked about the characteristics of a community and the process by which communities grow more intimate and meaningful. Four of us, Kathryn Larisey, Kathryn McCormick, Joan Savage, and I, decided to give it a try. We would meet weekly on Tuesday mornings for breakfast and talk about Jesus. In the process, we would try to apply some of Peck's thoughts on community and watch how our little experiment developed. Kathryn Larisey eventually moved to Atlanta and other folks came and went from the group, but the Three Musketeers were a constant. Eventually Sam and Janet Roberts joined us as stalwart members. When we all decided to move our meetings to Sam and Janet's home on Monday mornings—well, you can see the reason for the name change.

The amazing thing about this whole experiment was that we were able to get below the surface on a number of topics, not the least of which was who Jesus was when he was in his earthly ministry. The more we discussed the issue, the more compelling the search for answers became, until eventually we decided to hold a class at St. John's on—you guessed it—Jesus.

An important aspect of community cropped up within a little group that had been initiated by Frank Larisey, Kathryn's husband and associate rector of St. John's, called the Spiritual Growth Committee. Our task was to offer a number of spiritual experiences to the congregation. We eventually came up with two ideas that we managed to put into

8 M. Scott Peck, *The Different Drum: Community Making and Peace* (New York: Simon and Schuster, 1987).

effect: quiet days and the Maundy Thursday vigil. A quiet day, as we saw it, was a Saturday on which we met around 9:00 a.m. Beginning with the Service of Morning Prayer,[9] a meditation offered by one of the leaders of the quiet day would follow, which was itself followed by a period of quiet for prayer and reflection. A second and third meditation would be offered, each followed by quiet time, and the day would end with a communal lunch. This experience pointed out the importance of prayer in the life of any community of faith. Without a lively and spiritually mature prayer life, a community devolves into either a social group or an intellectual discussion group. If Jesus Christ is to remain at the center of the community of faith, a prayerful posture must be understood and nurtured at all times. The Spiritual Growth Committee was all about what that posture looks like and how to expose folks to the deep fruits of this posture. This nurturing process involves not only the frequency of prayer, but also the *style* of communal prayer. While this style can vary greatly, its form can have a profound effect on the life of the community. We will talk more about this below.

The Maundy Thursday vigil was another offspring of the Spiritual Growth Committee. The term "Maundy" is particularly interesting. It is an English term believed to be derived from the first word of the Latin phrase, *"Mandatum novum do vobis ut diligatis invicem sicut dilexi vos."* The connection to our discussion here is that it is the phrase spoken by Jesus in the Gospel of John (13:34), "A new commandment I

---

9 For those of you who are not Episcopalians, it is a service that can be led by any layperson, since it does not involve the offering of the Holy Eucharist. Early in my life, Episcopalians typically would offer Morning Prayer three out of four Sundays of the month with the fourth reserved for Holy Communion. Now Communion is generally done at every major Sunday and weekday service.

give to you, that you love one another as I have loved you."
As you will see, this new commandment is the whole point
of the community of faith and the theme of this book. In
other traditions it is known as Holy Thursday, but no matter
what you call it, it refers to the night and following day that
Jesus was dragged from authority to authority until he was
finally sentenced to crucifixion by Pontius Pilate. The vigil
has particular significance for two reasons. First, it was on
this night that Jesus prayed in the Garden of Gethsemane and
asked those who accompanied him to watch and wait while
he prayed.

> Then Jesus went with them to a place called
> Gethsem'ane, and he said to his disciples, "Sit
> here, while I go yonder and pray." And taking
> with him Peter and the two sons of Zeb'edee,
> he began to be sorrowful and troubled. Then he
> said to them, "My soul is very sorrowful, even
> to death; remain here, and watch with me."
> And going a little farther he fell on his face and
> prayed, "My Father, if it be possible, let this cup
> pass from me; nevertheless, not as I will, but as
> thou wilt." And he came to the disciples and
> found them sleeping; and he said to Peter, "So,
> could you not watch with me one hour? Watch
> and pray that you may not enter into temptation;
> the spirit indeed is willing, but the flesh is weak."
> Again, for the second time, he went away and
> prayed, "My Father, if this cannot pass unless I
> drink it, thy will be done." And again he came
> and found them sleeping, for their eyes were
> heavy. So, leaving them again, he went away and

prayed for the third time, saying the same words. Then he came to the disciples and said to them, "Are you still sleeping and taking your rest? Behold, the hour is at hand, and the Son of man is betrayed into the hands of sinners. Rise, let us be going; see, my betrayer is at hand." (Matt 26:36–46)

"Remain here and watch with me." There are few of us who do not feel a deep sadness at the failure of the disciples to fulfill this simplest of requests. You don't have to share my fate. You don't have to suffer or die, but could you just remain here and keep me company? It is this request that draws us to watch and wait in the church on the night of Maundy Thursday. We watch and wait until the noon service on Good Friday when Jesus was crucified.

The deep connection between being willing to do the simplest of tasks—watching and waiting—and the great gift of Jesus' love on that night binds together two critical aspects of the community of faith: the idea of attentiveness and the idea that love is at the center of all we do as Christians. Most of what we do as followers of Jesus Christ stems from some form of attentiveness. If we are not paying attention, we will never see the opportunities that are laid before us to love one another. It is through paying attention that we see—anything. The Maundy Thursday vigil is simply a powerful reminder of our obligation to *pay attention*. This idea that paying attention is a central part of any spiritual journey goes all the way back to the Old Testament in which Isaiah says, "pay attention so that you may live."[10]

---

10 "Incline your ear, and come to me; hear, that your soul may live." (Isa 55:3)

Second, the vigil reminds us of the love that was showered on us that night. As we sit quietly or pray, we cannot help but reflect on what he was going through for our sake—the hatred, the mocking, and the physical pain that ultimately ended on the Cross. The great mystery of God incarnate suffering for our sins is deeply reflected in the actions we take on Maundy Thursday and the vigil we keep. The nature of the community of faith is reflected not only by the power of his love for us, but also our own individual willingness to watch, wait, and pay attention.

It was during this time of considerable activity at St. John's that a change in leadership relieved me of some of my responsibilities and gave me the opportunity to roam. I recall meeting a friend, David Johnston, from the Concerned Citizens against Legalized Gambling (my one and only crusade) who was also the pastor of what would eventually become the Longtown Wesleyan Church. I mentioned to him my interest in the idea that we as Christians are called to be transformed into the likeness of Jesus Christ and my frustration concerning the difficulty of communicating that message. He suggested that the Wesleyan Church preached that message all the time.

And with that, I was off on another adventure in faith.

7

THE WESLEYANS

Not knowing anything about the Wesleyans—but trusting the down-to-earth character of David—I decided to visit. It was a small congregation of not more than seventy families. It was in many ways typical of the numerous small parishes dotting the southern landscape. What attracted me immediately was the intimacy of the congregation. Everyone knew each other, and therefore, everyone recognized me as someone new. I was showered with attention and enthusiastic care. It was as if I were a space alien who had just arrived from another planet, and everyone was curious about who I was and why I came. The reception was charming. I was definitely enticed to come back for more of whatever it was they were dishing out.

The Wesleyans, who take their name from John Wesley, the founder of the Methodists, branched off from the Methodist Episcopal Church around the time of the American Civil War (also known as *The War Between the States* for moderate southerners or *The War for Southern Independence* for those more devout or *The War of Northern Aggression* for those of an even more rabid variety). As in so many Christian churches, slavery was a central area of contention. In the late 1700s, the Methodists had adopted an anti-slavery position, but found it hard to enforce, especially with the influential southern contingent so violently opposed to the position. Those who were staunch abolitionists found it more difficult to hold sway in this contentious environment. In 1843, the Wesleyan Methodist Connection was officially formed at a gathering of anti-slavery ministers and laymen in Utica, New York. Since their theology and ethics tended to result from a stricter interpretation of Scripture, they tended to be relatively conservative Methodists who insisted that the church oppose slavery. This more conservative interpretation shows itself today in the centrality of Scripture, the emphasis on holiness as a natural goal of all Christian life, and in the more strict observance of Sunday as the Lord's Day. They go to church on Sunday morning for their normal worship service and Sunday school, and then return in the evening for a prayer service. They do not, in general, go golfing or water skiing on Sunday, but gather for the Sunday noon meal as a central expression of family and community. They also gather on Wednesday evenings for prayer and teaching.

A more wonderful, warm, and generous group of folks one could never meet. I was smitten. Again, knowing the pastor was a quick way to integrate into congregational life, and I ended up teaching an adult Sunday school class and directing the choir. I would also go to the pastor's home on Sundays for the noon meal. I recall fondly sitting at the kitchen table peeling apples for the ubiquitous apple pie. We would relax, talk, sing songs, and maybe watch some football on TV until it was time to return to church for the Sunday evening prayer service.

One of the more interesting experiences I had was directing the choir. I had mentioned to Elizabeth Davis, one of the choir members, that I was singing in a large chorus for men—The Palmetto Mastersingers. At that point she asked if I would be willing to help them. I protested that I did not play the piano, to which she said they had plenty of piano players but no one who knew how to run a choir. On this basis, I allowed as how I certainly was willing to meet with them and offer any assistance I could. When we met for the first time, she introduced me as the great white hope and asked me to tell them where they should sit. Oh boy, now what?

One little voice in my head told me that I really was not equipped to do this, and another little voice said, *Of course you are. Tell them where to sit, dummy.* OK, well the sopranos and altos over here and the tenors and basses over here. And with that we were off and running. None of the members had ever sung in an organized choir before (as far as I knew) and most could not read choral music, so we started singing simple four-part harmony from the hymnal. Eventually it got to be Christmas time and we needed to pick something for a special choir program. This was my introduction to the "cantata." Much of this kind of music is sort of drippy, but I talked with a gentleman at Brodt Music Company in Charlotte, North Carolina, and we settled on a lovely piece. We practiced and practiced until we managed to execute it pretty well. I had been the student conductor of my high school band, so at least I had some conducting exposure. All in all, it was a remarkable experience—learning, struggling, and eventually achieving a lovely harmony I like to believe was reflective in some small degree of the harmony in heaven, whatever that harmony might look like. We did this *together.*

There was a "we" held together by our common desire to serve God and the congregation.

Finally, I was asked to teach the adult Sunday school class. Now remember, I really am not a Wesleyan—I am a transplanted Episcopalian/former Methodist/former Baptist. But for some reason they trusted me. They trusted me to care about them, and they trusted me to care about our faith. Here was an opportunity, just as with every other teaching situation, to model the process of combining teaching and participating. What we did, we did *together*. There was much dialogue and questioning and even challenging one another. I recall asking the question, "Who is the model for our faith?" and the discussion centered on Jesus (of course). One of the members of the class, who was a religion major at the local Bible college, suggested that Jesus didn't need faith in the normal sense of the word. I must admit, it was only years later that I more fully appreciated the subtle issues at stake in that discussion, but there we were having it in our little Sunday school class in my little Wesleyan church. We could disagree and at the same time trust the love of Christ that was always implicit in our gathering. While often we think that preserving equanimity by avoiding conflict is the norm of church communities, this model of open dialogue founded on trust has become central to my understanding of an even higher calling within the community of faith.

Let me offer one more episode regarding the choir. A teenage girl wanted desperately to sing in the choir because her mother was a member, and we seemed to be having a lot of fun (which we were). It certainly was a little community within a community. There was only one problem—she couldn't carry a tune in a bucket. She was a wonderful artist and a lovely person—she had many talents—but she couldn't

find a note if she and it were alone on a very small desert island. A choral singer was not who she was created to be.

Now some of us have talents in some areas and some have
talents in other areas. Few of us are talented in everything,
and it behooves us to learn what our strengths and weaknesses are and not impose our weaknesses on others. Here is the
dilemma: *how are love and truth best served?* We tend to believe
that church choirs are something different from other musical
organizations. All we need to do is to "make a joyful noise,"
and not only God but also the congregation will be infinitely
indulgent. How can we justify asking someone *not* to be in
the choir, if we as Christians are called to be kind and generous? Consequently our church choirs are filled with folks
who have—let us say—other talents. Well, here is an alternative interpretation. Communities of faith are places where
love *and* truth reign. Love without truth is a sham and truth
without love is cruelty. Sometimes the most loving thing to
do in the long run is to stick to the truth with love. In other
words, I am laying the groundwork here for my actions. And
you guessed it—I told the youngster she could not be in the
choir. No one else understood such an "un-Christian" thing
to do, but here is the point: the community of faith is where
love *and* truth collide, get integrated, and shine forth as an
immutable whole. It is not the place where untruth is en-
abled. All too often, we enable a lie in the name of charity,
when in fact it is not charity at all but our own selfish un-
willingness to take the heat for living into the truth. Consequently, the choir, the congregation, and maybe even God
suffer the excruciating indignity of poorly executed music.
Now you are probably saying, "You didn't!" Yes, I did. But I
hope she can look back on this experience as I do and chuckle. I still love her dearly and hope I did not scar her for life. In

fact, it may seem that the issues of encouraging participation and not enabling delusion are in conflict. How can we see as our goal to offer opportunities for folks to grow and at the same time tell them that they can't participate? That is a good question and the answer is subtle and yet important. What we are about is encouraging folks to grow in love and truth. As we said, love without truth is a sham, and truth without love is cruelty. To keep these in balance may be the job of the Holy Spirit acting in and through the decisions we as leaders and we as members of a congregation make regarding our paths toward Christ's likeness.

So what does my experience with the Wesleyans tell us about the community of faith? First of all, smaller congregations offer the best opportunity for all the members to know one another—to sit next to folks you know, to sing with folks you know, to pray with folks you know, and to be on a common journey toward likeness in Christ with folks you know. In addition, the only way folks are going to recognize *new people* is for them to know the *old people*. If you don't know the people who worship with you every week, then how in the world are you going to know when someone new to the congregation wanders in? New people come for a wide variety of reasons, but one thing is almost certain—you only get one shot at receiving them with the love of Christ. If they don't feel well received there is no reason whatsoever for them to return. Unlike Catholics, Protestants do not feel an overarching obligation to go to church once a week. If they don't want to go, they don't. Somehow, if we want them to return, it is incumbent upon us to make newcomers feel welcome and have some mechanism for them to plug into the community—the first day you meet them. If you fail, it may be the last day you see them. This little Wesleyan community successfully did just that for me.

Second, communities of faith are open to folks offering their gifts. Here I was, the new kid on the block, directing the choir and teaching Sunday school within a year or so of my arrival. There was no territorial possessiveness. All they wanted to do was worship their Lord, learn, and offer their gifts. At the same time, though, the community of faith is a place where we work out how to love in truth and to live the truth with love. This is not always easy. The conflicts that arise are emblematic of the eternal struggle between light and darkness. A community of faith that does not struggle is probably one that is not growing in faith. I can't quite express enough my deep thanks to the Wesleyans for the gift of love *and* truth they showed me. My life has been enriched beyond measure because of them. As seems to be the rhythm of my life, however, there came a time to move on. I felt it was time to return to St. John's and see what had been happening during my three-year hiatus with the Wesleyans.

8

THE EPISCOPALIANS—III

When I returned to St. John's, I was gratified at being well received. I had numerous good friends there, and I was comfortable to be in what felt like a familiar old coat. I had no desire to take on any leadership responsibilities, not that anyone was breaking down my door with offers. Upon Alan Avery's retirement, the rectorship fell to Fletcher Montgomery. Fletcher was a convert to Anglicanism—his father was a Presbyterian minister—and his approach to liturgy and theology had a unique and "eclectic" patina that made him an effective pastor. It was during this period, that the idea emerged from the Tuesday Morning Breakfast Club to develop an adult Sunday school class with the theme of radical Christian transformation. We had been casting about for a title for the course when I mentioned that we could only scratch the surface of the topic. At this point, Joan Savage suggested that we call the class "Scratching the Surface of Christian Transformation." Done! We were off and running. We met several times to block out the scope of the class and to gather materials. Basically it was centered on a series of readings from a variety of authors, the central point of which was that we are called into a radical transformation into the likeness of Jesus Christ. Ultimately, we began with a solid group of folks who would participate in our inaugural effort, and I think everyone was to some extent enlightened by this introduction. Some were more comfortable with the ideas we explored than others, but at least we got the concepts out on the table. After the class, no one could say that they had never heard such radical thinking. Now, let me make this clear. Here was a little group of Episcopalians leading this course who only had the brief catechism in the back of the *Book of Common Prayer* to go on and our own instincts— instincts that were being formed by our little community of faith—the Tuesday Morning Breakfast Club. Out of this came the earth shaking realization that Jesus came here to offer us *all of himself.*

Somewhere in the process, I wrote down a set of questions about Jesus, entitled "A Little Christian Quiz," and asked our rector, Fletcher Montgomery, if he would answer them. This story is mostly covered in the book I would eventually write, entitled *The Quiz: On the Nature of the Incarnation of Jesus Christ.*[11] The course was essentially a process of finding an-swers to the questions on the quiz. At this point, all we knew for certain was that what we were teaching was consistent with our understanding of Anglican Christology. We were dependent on the idea that truth is available to those who seek, but the seeking probably needs to be more intense than merely showing up at church once a week. It took a fledgling community of faith, the Tuesday Morning Breakfast Club, to enable the deep discernment process to start to take place. For this opportunity, I will be eternally grateful to Kathryn

11 Denver: St Maximus Scriptorium, 2012.

Larisey, Kathryn McCormick, and Joan Savage for starting the whole process off.

At some point after having taught "Scratching" a number of times at St. John's, I realized that I had played that tune enough and should either play another tune or find another street corner. The only Episcopal priest I knew who made what I considered to be "a perfect score" on *The Quiz* was Blaney Pridgen, so I called him and made an appointment to visit with him. I knew that we were singing from the same sheet of music. He was rector of St. Mary's Episcopal Church on the other side of Columbia from St. John's. At this meeting we agreed to teach the course together, so off I went on another adventure. We really had a wonderful time. We had between fifteen and twenty people that first year, and the active participation of the rector was an important draw. We actually started out with *The Quiz* as a method of engaging folks with some fundamental questions about Jesus, ones that would be addressed in the course. One of the most interesting aspects of the course was our ability to disagree. We had some good dialogue in which all the participants, including the rector, took part. This was another stunning example of a leader as participant. I taught the course a second year without the participation of the rector and found once again that interest was limited. It was time to return to what seemed to be my home base—St. John's. One of the things I took away with me, however, was the love and encouragement of all those I encountered at St. Mary's. I met some lasting friends (some of whom I still owe money) and cherish the experience.

It was through the process of developing the content for "Scratching the Surface of Christian Transformation" that I ran head first into the Catholic understanding of who Jesus was. I had called two Catholic professors of Christology at two different Catholic seminaries and asked them if they had time to answer a few questions about Jesus—yep—*The Quiz.* Both graciously took the time to talk with me, and both gave very similar answers to the questions. While I had asked many ministers to answer the questions, Sister Sarah Butler of Mundelein Seminary outside of Chicago and Father Gregory Carruthers of St. Augustine's Seminary in Toronto, Canada gave the most consistent answers. Neither one hesitated (well, maybe a little) and offered profound answers to each of the questions. Eventually, as a result of my initial contact with Fr. Carruthers, I spent a week with him at St. Augustine's. He and I would walk across the beautiful campus on the Scarborough Bluffs—high above Lake Ontario—and talk at length about a number of issues that influence the way we understand who Jesus was. While there, I also attended a series of talks and homilies given by retired Archbishop Adam Exner from Vancouver, British Columbia. Almost the first words out of his mouth were a call to be transformed into the likeness of Jesus Christ. I felt I was home. Both of these experiences—the conversations with Fr. Carruthers and the talks given by Archbishop Exner—led me to consider, ever so gingerly, the remote possibility of "swimming the Tiber," as some Protestants refer to the process of becoming Roman Catholic. I felt that in the gentleness and kindness of Fr. Carruthers, I had seen the face of Christ. In the thoughtful deliberations of Archbishop Exner, I had seen the best of the Catholic deposit of faith. It was just what we had been talking about in our classes on radical transformation. I had a chance to sit down and talk with Archbishop Exner on several occasions over the week, and his generosity and transparency reflected to me the very best of the Christian person—one for whom love *and* truth were paramount.[12]

Upon returning from my Toronto experience, I vowed to do all in my power to elevate my commitment to teach Catholic/Anglican Christology (the study of Christ) to Episcopalians. To accomplish this, I made an appointment to see the Bishop of the Episcopal Diocese of Upper South Carolina, Dorsey Henderson. I took the manuscript I had been using for my course with me to my appointment and talked with the Bishop about the idea that Anglicans had never repudiated basic Catholic teaching on Jesus, to which he heartily agreed. I told him that I would like to take this course out into the diocese with his blessing, at which point he asked the Canon to the Ordinary,[13] Michael Bullock, to join us. The Bishop's opening comment to Father Bullock was, "Michael, Jonathan wants to talk about *Jesus*." He was right on the money. We had a fruitful discussion and the Bishop said that he would send my materials around to see what might be developed. I appreciated his efforts, but after a subsequent conversation with Michael, I felt as if I were getting no traction. On the way home I was passing St. Joseph Catholic Church, and I turned right—right into the parking lot. This was to be the beginning of my first committed encounter with the Catholics.

---

12 I have to tell this little story, but I really need to place it here in a note. While I was at the seminary in Toronto, I noticed that the soap in the shower was *Irish Spring*. I couldn't help but remark to Abp. Exner: "Now, don't let anyone tell you that the Catholics are not sneaky—puttin' a bar of *Irish Spring* in the shower. As I washed, a bit of an Irish jig began to creep into my movement—and then I started to sing a few bars of Christmas in Killarney—and I became mar and mar Cath'lic with every scroob." I loved his delightful laughter at my little tale.

13 The Canon to the Ordinary is the Bishop's assistant, in this case responsible for the development of faith and teaching in the diocese.

9

THE CATHOLICS

I marched right up to the front desk of the parish offices and asked to see the pastor. I was then directed to his secretary who gave me an appointment for the following Wednesday. When I sat down with Father Richard Harris, I began by telling him a little of my story and how I had arrived at this point in my spiritual journey. I then talked specifically about my interest in our radical transformation into the likeness of Jesus Christ. As you might have noticed, I had at that point become a one-trick pony, a one-hit wonder, a one-tune trumpet player who simply changes street corners. He smiled and nodded. He was right with me. When I finished my dissertation, he just smiled and said, "Well, if you want to do this, *welcome.*" I don't want to be too mushy here, but my eyes filled with tears (again?). I had found a theological home. I then asked him what it would take for me to become a Catholic. He described the process called the Rite of Christian Initiation for Adults, or RCIA, and suggested that I might want to try that and see how it felt. *Okay*, I thought, *I'm in.*

RCIA is a thirty-week course in Catholicism. It really is unlike anything I had experienced in my sampling of other churches. There are two aspects of Catholicism that are most clear to those on the outside: you are not allowed to take communion if you are not a Catholic and, maybe less obvious but not surprising, it is not easy to become a Catholic. The closest training I have experienced is the Episcopal inquirers class. Since I was a cradle Episcopalian, I never took it, but I have helped teach aspects of it a number of times. RCIA is a bit more formal because there is so much more to understand: church history going back two thousand years, church structure, sacramental meaning and protocols, theology and its implications for a number of current issues, and so on. While the cradle Catholics may not know much of this stuff, the initiates get a large dose. In many cases, cradle Catholics will attend RCIA classes as a refresher, if not an out-and-out introduction. The one thing that stood out in my experience was that it was a consistent group of about eighteen people who met every Tuesday evening to go over and discuss extensive handouts on the various subjects being covered. We began with prayer, and we ended with prayer. We knew each other's names, we shared our journeys, we discussed our understanding of difficult topics, and we had a common goal—to cross the finish line at the Easter Vigil service on the following Easter Eve. In other words, we were a little community of faith.

As an Episcopalian, I was up on most of the sacramental and liturgical basics and so could concentrate on the subtle and not-so-subtle differences. For example, for Episcopalians, a sacrament is an outward and visible sign of an inward and spiritual grace. For Catholics, a sacrament is an *efficacious* sign of an inward and spiritual grace. The *sign* actually *brings* the grace. By analogy it would be as if the flag on the mailbox is not just a sign that the mail is in the box—but the flag *put it there!* These kinds of differences were intriguing to me and supported in every way the theology that I had come to appreciate as the fundamentals of Jesus Christ and his Incarnation. Here is another one. For Episcopalians, the Holy Eucharist, the bread eaten at the celebration of Holy Communion, embodies the "real presence" of Jesus Christ. It is actually not Jesus until you consume it. For Catholics, once the bread is consecrated, *it IS Jesus*—the body, blood, soul, and divinity of Jesus Christ. That makes the implications a bit less subtle. Out of this understanding we get Augustine's admonishment, "Be who you are and *become* what you eat."[14] For me, that was a tremendous reinforcement of the entire radical transformation theme. It is all there in one form or another, popping its head up in liturgy, sacraments, theology, and even church structure.

If we were to take seriously the idea that individual Christians are called to be perfectly Christ-like, then why would we be surprised that some managed to exhibit those characteristics? The Church calls them saints. Now, I don't intend for this to be an apologetic for the Catholic Church. I hope many who are reading this are not Catholics. The challenge here is to get to the basics of our Christian journey that apply to us all—and particularly those basics that inform our understanding of the community of faith—for *all* of us.

I was received into the Catholic Church at the Easter Vigil

---

14 The Latin is "*Estote quod videtis, et accipite quod estis,*" which literally would be translated, "Be what you see; receive what you eat." It seems to be a bit of a play on words. The above paraphrase, which captures more simply the deep transformative meaning, was offered to me by my pastor, Fr. Álvaro Montero.

service on April 2, 2009. It really was a glorious service and
quite moving. I won't go into any details except to say that
each aspect of the service reinforced the very reasons why I
was there. At that point, I knew that my decision to "swim
the Tiber" was a good one—at least for me at this stage of
my journey. I was a committed—and probably an obnox-
iously enthusiastic—*Catholic*. But now what? What I discovered next was just as important as what I had learned up to
that point: *becoming* a Catholic is much different than *being* a
Catholic. This book has a lot to do with this distinction.

While we continued to have RCIA classes after we were
received, eventually they ceased and I was left without my
little community of faith. Some went to different Catholic parishes, some went to other masses than I did, and still
others were just swallowed up into the large hoard of other Catholics attending the same mass I did. There was no
Sunday school for adults after mass, and we had coffee and
doughnuts only once a month, at which time we just stood
around and chatted. Many would get their doughnut and just
go home. *Ugh!* I felt particularly alone as a single guy in his
sixties. It was at this point that I started to think seriously
about the idea of a community of faith and what it might
mean for me and my fellow travelers.

I left Columbia, South Carolina for Clarkesville, Georgia
after having experienced the massive downturn in the econ-
omy and a concomitant downturn in my consulting work.
I sold my house and much of its contents and moved into a
huge two thousand-square-foot apartment in the house of
a dear friend, Bob Muldoon, and joined St. Mark Catholic
Church in Clarkesville. This was a much smaller parish than
St. Joseph in Columbia, and there was only one main "An-
glo" service on Sunday. Consequently, when we gathered

after mass in the large meeting room adjacent to the church, we effectively were meeting with most of the folks who had just attended the service. Here was community—of a sort. No Sunday school as I had known it, but certainly community. As I grew to know the members of the parish, I began to talk about the possibility of having a class of some kind after mass.

Just about the time I was to try to put this idea into action, Bob told me that he was thinking about selling the house and moving to Florida. This was clearly a great move for him, and I was very encouraging. The next morning I was sitting in my living room thinking about the conversation the night before and thought to myself, *Okay, little Mr. Encouragement, what in the world are you going to do?* It took me about 3.7 seconds to come to the conclusion: *I know exactly what I'm going to do—I'm going back to Denver.* Of course this involved packing up again for the second time in a year and planning the extensive logistics of getting stuff in storage, furniture moved by United Van Lines, and hauling the rest of my stuff—along with my car—out to Denver, but I managed to pull it off. I found myself in a thousand-square-foot apartment on Mineral Avenue in Littleton, just south of Metropolitan Denver. Every time I drove west over C470 and caught the first glimpse of the Front Range, I had to pinch myself. I finally felt at home geographically. But what about a church?

The closest one to me was St. Mary Catholic Parish, so I started attending there. I think the most memorable aspect of my early attendance was that no one said hello. Now I am not pointing the finger at St Mary's. This is a common problem with many large congregations. As I mentioned above, how can you know who is new if you don't know who is old? The beginning of this process of knowing "who is old"

67

is to start *paying attention*. Our failure to do this does not appear, on the surface, to be an integral part of our Christian walk. We go to mass. Our children attend Catholic school. We make regular contributions to the church's coffers. I even say hello to the priests. What is this *paying attention* gig?

Recall the Maundy Thursday Vigil. "Watch and wait with me." Paying attention may just be the very foundation of everything we do as Christians. If we are called to love, how are we to know who and when and where to love if we are not paying attention? If we are called to proclaim the truth of the Gospel, how are we to know to whom and when and where to proclaim that truth if we are not paying attention. Looking up and paying attention is the very heart and soul of the community of faith, and, sadly, most Christian parishes often miss the boat. It is easy if you are small, because you are always confronted with folks you know. Larger parishes, on the other hand, are more challenging because you are always confronted with folks you don't know. Even if everyone picks a service and sticks to it, the sheer number of people militates for anonymity. Now, *what is wrong with a little anonymity,* you might say? *I like to go to church and be quiet and unwind.* Well, unwinding is fine, but not essentially Christian. What is essentially Christian is the admonition to love one another as we have been loved. Somehow we need to know how to do that in the context of a large parish. Furthermore, the propensity not to pick a service and stick with it further compounds the problem. To the extent that we bounce from service to service, even from church to church, is precisely the degree to which we block the possibility of becoming a true community of faith. Unfortunately, this was my experience with the Catholics—not enough paying attention and too much bouncing. The fact that we had no adult Sunday school was the final nail in the communal coffin. We had coffee and doughnuts after mass almost every week, so in that sense, there was a great opportunity to develop community, but the culture was not one that fostered a discussion of our faith. Mostly it was just an opportunity to chat with friends and occasionally to meet people you may or may not ever see again. It may look like I am bashing my own faith community, but in reality every church to some extent suffers from these kinds of symptoms, so I am trying to lay the groundwork for what follows.

One practice that was instituted at St. Mary's was a Welcoming Committee, out of which came the thrust to organize greeters for each mass. At least if you were a greeter, you would get to see the folks at your mass who were consistent in their attendance, and if you took the time, you could learn some folks' names. There is a lovely older lady named Lucille whom I would sing to each week—"You picked a fine time to leave me Lucille; four hungry children and a crop in the field."[15] Now, there is a bond! I think she actually looked forward to seeing me—and I her. We were starting to have a stake in attending that particular mass, and that is the start of real community.

While the presence or absence of Sunday school, the habit of paying attention, and the propensity to bounce around from mass to mass or from church to church are cultural and can be solved by good leadership, there are other more recalcitrant obstacles to community that seem to be particular to the Catholic Church. Let me mention a few. Catholics feel—and rightly so—that the best education we can give our Catholic children is one that is grounded in the Catholic

15 Kenny Rogers, lyrics by Joe Turner, © EMI Music Publishing, Sony/ ATV Music Publishing LLC, Universal Music Publishing Group.

faith. We like, as much as possible, to educate our children in Catholic schools. This would be true for any faith—Episcopal children in Episcopal schools, Baptist children in Baptist schools, etc. In fact, I spent my first and second grade years in a Catholic school and my fourth, fifth, and sixth grades in an Episcopal school. Parochial schools are a good thing. My sophomore, junior, and senior high school years were spent in the public school system—which was also a good thing, but for different reasons. Sometimes the opportunities to play certain sports or to play in the marching band are only available in public schools. The interesting phenomenon that presents itself in the Catholic culture is that those who go to Catholic school usually receive their religious training in school. Those who go to public schools or non-Catholic private schools have to receive their religious training in Sunday school—usually called CCD, which stands for the imposing name Confraternity of Christian Doctrine. In other words, Sunday school is only designed for a portion of the children in the parish. The division between the children who do go to Sunday school and those who don't immediately divides the congregation into the parents of children who "do" and the parents of children who "don't". This division results in certain parents and children leaving mass right after the service and other parents having to hang around while their children receive their religious training in Sunday school. Now, each parish handles the logistics of this differently, but almost universally the division is there and is hard to overcome.

Another challenge is that Catholic churches often are constructed with two major focuses: the mass and the school. Therefore, they often have a church building, an office building, and a school building. In general, large parish facilities for Sunday school are simply not constructed. Thus, if one wanted to hold a Sunday school class for adults after a particular mass, the first challenge would be where to hold it. One of the most refractory problems in building community may, therefore, have to do with bricks and mortar. In general, Protestant churches build Sunday school facilities that can accommodate all grade levels—as well as adults. Space, while it may not be adequate for a congregation that is growing, is always seen as an essential part of the life of the church community, and leadership is constantly planning for the needed expansion. The Catholic culture seems not to be driven by the same concerns.

AND YOUR POINT WOULD BE?

The point here is not to accuse, but to understand the current state of affairs and to try to address it. It should also be stated that it is doubtful that Jesus would be perfectly pleased with any of us—Protestant or Catholic. Even though we may not have the same barriers to a full community of faith, the chances are very good that we all fail to some degree to use the opportunities we have been given to their full potential. One of the objectives of this book is to show all of us—myself included—how we might see a more complete picture of the community of faith that Jesus would recognize as that of his disciples—one that is centered on love.

The preceding chapters have been about my personal experiences in a variety of communities of faith. The assumption here is that these personal experiences have validity not only for me as an individual, but also may have broader validity for all of us that share the same humanity. This is a bold assumption, but one that seems to be confirmed as we read the works of theologians such as Henri de Lubac, apologists such as C. S. Lewis, and mystical writers such as Therese of Lisieux. These thinkers have the ability to draw from within themselves, see connections, and organize their experiences in such a way that they have universal meaning. The conclusions that follow come largely from my own experiences, and yet I have the audacity to believe that there just might be embedded in these experiences something of universal value concerning the nature of the community of faith.

It is remarkable how our understanding of anything—love, compassion, truth, humor, wonder, beauty—is somehow imprinted on our very being. The way in which we take in experiences and organize them into some form of understanding is, to say the least, inspiring. It is like some sort of spiritual DNA. Christians would call that the *image of God*. While we are well aware of the concept, we understand little of how it works. If we use DNA as a metaphor and consider how it is used by our bodies to organize amino acids into complex protein "machines" that do a mind-boggling number of sophisticated tasks, we might think of our spiritual DNA as a template that helps us organize sensory inputs into meaningful experiences and understanding. What molecular biology has discovered about how the complex systems of the body function must leave all but the most ardent evolutionists in a state of awe.[16] If DNA itself can inspire in this way, how much more can the wonder of spiritual DNA, the image of God, inspire us and leave us in awe. The point here is to assert the possibility that there is something built into us as human beings that allows us, if we are open to the process, to tap into that image of God, our spiritual DNA, and to say

16 See Michael J. Behe, *Darwin's Black Box: The Biochemical Challenge to Evolution* (2d ed.; New York: Free Press, 2006), 329.

something of value—something that is true. It is unequivocal that I cannot be the judge of that value. All I can do is to be as open to the process as possible and pray that my own spiritual DNA has not been too corrupted by spiritual mutations (we might call that *sin*) as to lead to perverse conclusions.

In the parts that follow, I will try to set forth in a more systematic way my own understanding of the characteristics of a vital Christian community of faith and how such a community might be formed. The fundamental organizing principle that I believe is imprinted on our spiritual DNA is the love of Christ, the proof text being what I am calling the Eleventh Commandment.

PART II

THE CHRISTIAN COMMUNITY OF FAITH

10

THE ELEVENTH COMMANDMENT

A new commandment I give to you, that you love one another even as I have loved you.
John 13:34

By this all men will know that you are my disciples, if you have love for one another.
John 13:35

These two quotations from the Gospel of John are the driving force of all we do as Christians. The question that has challenged the Christian community from the first century up to today is: *How do we act this out?* How do we act this out among ourselves, within our respective expressions of our Christian faith in the vast variety of denominations, congregations, and parishes? How do we act this out with regard to our relationships with those outside our respective communities—both Christian and non-Christian—both people of faith and those whose "faith" is expressed in family, work, service, or recreation? What aspects of our faith influence how we act toward those close to us and those whom we briefly encounter as we wend our way through our daily lives? To approach these questions, we should start by understanding something of the way these portions of Scripture fit into the larger picture of Jesus' ministry on earth—the Incarnation. We then must look at the concept of love and try to flesh out its variety of interpretations and expressions. This discussion must include the way in which the Holy Trinity embodies our understanding of the relationship between the Son and the Father and the nature of the love that binds them. Once we have done this, we can dive into the way these ideas form a foundation for our understanding of the community of faith—how they influence the way we gather, the way we sing, the way we pray, the way we play, the way we talk with one another, the way we are or are not involved in each other's struggles and joy, and the way we share our journeys and the basis of those journeys, the Gospel, among ourselves and with others.

This *walking together* is really the crux of the matter. Understanding a common goal and experiencing a rich community of faith as we move toward that goal is what Christianity is all about. All too often, however, we think that the structural elements of our faith—the liturgy, worship, programs, committees and ministries, and the relationships that naturally flow from these—are sufficient. We often are not deliberate in the way we view the importance of the community and the way we structure it. Whatever happens communally is often spontaneous, sporadic, or for many, even nonexistent. Some have been "cradle" Christians and have wandered away because they failed to see their Christian experience as compelling enough to view it as essential to their fullness of life. Others have come to a church only to drift away because there has not been anything of substance that they could easily grasp in order to give them a sense of value. Finally, there are many who never come to any church because their view from the *outside* never gives them a sense of something compelling going on *inside*. The challenge for all Christians, independent of our specific tradition, is to be a light—a light not only to those within our respective congregations, but also a light to those outside—a light that is so attractive that all who see it will want to know more of its warmth and life-giving spirit.

To place the *new commandment* of Jesus in John 13 into some kind of perspective we must at some level look at a broader picture of his *mission* on earth. I will try to keep this simple and not develop a number of theological issues that could form stumbling blocks (both to me and you) to a clear understanding of my thesis. Jesus was a Jew born into a modest family in first century Palestine. His training in what we Christians call the Old Testament—the Hebrew Tanak, which includes the Torah, the Prophets, and the Writings—was thorough.[17] While he was always the one who had come from heaven to save the world, the Son of God, he "increased in wisdom and in stature, and in favor with God and man" (Luke 2:52). We can thus assume that his understanding of his mission also grew until it blossomed at age thirty. We, of course, can ask what in the world he was doing for those first thirty years, and we can assume that he was learning and growing and coming to some conclusions about the failure of the Jewish establishment to live into the promises inherent

---

17 The **TaNaK** is really an acronym that is made up of the three letters that begin the three sections of the Hebrew Bible: the **T**orah, the **N**evi'im, or Prophets, and the **K**etuvim, or Writings.

in their own Scripture and, finally, he was struggling with his own call.

What this struggle actually looked like we will never know, but it is all too easy to downplay the possibility or importance of such a struggle. What we can say unequivocally is that this struggle continued all the way to the Garden of Gethsemane, when he was finally confronted by the inevitable prospect of his own crucifixion, and even to the cross where he appeared to struggle with his own abandonment by the Father.[18] How this journey conditioned his understanding of the Jewish failure and the remedies he prescribed is laid out both explicitly and implicitly in the Gospels. All of his teachings were designed to bring the Jewish people back into right relation to God. Even the very idea that a man could claim the intimate relationship with the Father that Jesus claimed implied something profound about the possible relationship of Jew and Gentile to God. How he addressed sin and forgiveness set a new benchmark for humanity. The idea that one could refrain from sin and thus be a child of God was most radical. The idea that the Kingdom of God was actually on display in the very person of Jesus pointed to the fact that the Kingdom of God was "at hand" (Matt 4:17) and available to all of us on earth. Moreover, the idea that the kingdom was even more accessible to those without power and influence turned the whole concept of righteousness on its head. Finally, the centrality of the concept of love set a new standard for the kind of life of which he spoke.

---

18 Of course, there is another explanation of his words that are found in Psalm 22, but we are taking a more straightforward approach here. No one can ever be certain what the correct interpretation is. There is no doubt, however, about the incredible power and emotion associated with the words, "E'lo-i, E'lo-i, la'ma sabach-tha'ni"—"My God, My God, why hast thou forsaken me?"

The Jewish tradition as reflected in her Scripture was based on the story of the Jewish people. At every turn they were asked to *remember.* The stories of Adam and Eve, Noah, Moses, Abraham, Joseph, Isaac, Jacob, Jonah, Ruth, David, and on and on form the foundation of the Jewish understanding of life. In particular, the several covenants formed throughout this history laid out the way God related to his people.[19] Life was found in being in right relationship with the creator God—the wholly other God who entered into history through acts of aid, mercy, and wrath in order to correct the people of God and help them to see their lives only in terms of a total dependence on him. There were theophanies, like the burning bush or the angel of God wrestling with Jacob, but God had never before shown up as a human being. The Writings, such as the historical books (Chronicles and Kings), Psalms, and Proverbs, taught the people of God their history and the ways of righteousness. The Prophets spoke of those who rose up again and again to correct the path the people were on by warning them of the consequences of their ways. All of this religious culture became the foundation upon which Jesus formed his understanding of the will of the Father for him and upon which he built his teaching. For the Jewish people of his day, he was a troublemaker. For modern Jews, he is considered by many to have been a prophet—one who was sent to correct their deviation from the way of God. As Christians, of course, we would say he was much more, but we should recognize that his roots and his self-understanding cannot be appreciated apart from his Jewish faith. As he said, he did not come to abolish the law but to fulfill it (Matt 5:17). His faith was that of a first century Jew. His proclamation

---

19 The Old Testament Covenants include those with Adam, Noah, Abraham, Moses, and David. Jesus represents the New Covenant.

plumbed the depths of that faith, cleared away the extraneous aspects that had grown up over the centuries, and cut to the core of what it meant to follow the God of Abraham, Isaac, and Jacob. It was his mission to see with the eyes of God the true meaning of the Jewish faith—his own faith. In other words, there is no such thing as a "New Testament" Jesus who can be viewed independently from the "Old Testament" faith and law that formed him.

This law was centered on the Ten Commandments (the Decalogue or Ten Words) received by Moses on Mount Sinai (Exod 20:1–17 and Deut 5:6–21). While there were 613 "commandments" (or *mitzvot*) received from God and written in the books of the Torah, for the early Hebrew people the Ten Commandments were the ultimate benchmark of right behavior and right spiritual posture. Being in accord with these commandments offered the possibility of oneness with God—a profound accord with the will of God. The Ark of the Covenant, which held the tablets on which the Ten Commandments were written, was the centerpiece of Jewish worship. It was considered to be the seat of God and resided in the sanctuary of the Temple in Jerusalem—the Holy of Holies. Therefore, for Jesus to suggest that he was giving a *new commandment* was either the height of audacity or the absolute depth of revelation.

To appreciate what a new commandment might mean, we need to look at the "old" commandments and particularly their form. The first commandment admonishes the people to worship only the God of Abraham, Isaac, and Jacob—the God of Israel:

> I am the Lord your God, who brought you out of
> the land of Egypt, out of the house of bondage.

You shall have no other gods before me. (Deut 5:6–7)

The only other commandments that are positive are the ones to *observe and keep holy* the Sabbath day and to *honor* your father and mother. All the rest are negative in that they say, *you shall not.* When Jesus is asked, "Which is the greatest commandment?" he answers in the positive:

> But when the Pharisees heard that he had silenced the Sadducees, they came together. And one of them, a lawyer, asked him a question, to test him. "Teacher, which is the great commandment in the law?" And he said to him, "You shall love the Lord your God with all your heart, and with all your soul, and with all your mind. This is the great and first commandment. And a second is like it, You shall love your neighbor as yourself. On these two commandments depend all the law and the prophets." (Matt 22:34–40)

The Pharisees must have been stunned by the way in which Jesus turned things around and centered the whole Jewish faith on *love.* Nowhere in the Ten Commandments as presented in Exodus or Deuteronomy is the word *love* mentioned and yet evidently the Pharisees were silenced. They must have known deep inside that he was emphasizing the true meaning of the Jewish faith in a new way. But, where did he get these ideas about the love of God and neighbor? Were these ideas foreign to the Pharisees? Was this a new take on the meaning of the commandments?

Consider the following:

> . . . and you shall love the LORD your God with all your heart, and with all your soul, and with all your might. (Deut 6:5)

> You shall not hate your brother in your heart, but you shall reason with your neighbor, lest you bear sin because of him. You shall not take vengeance or bear any grudge against the sons of your own people, but you shall love your neighbor as yourself: I am the LORD. (Lev 19:17–18)

The most remarkable thing here is how Jesus draws these two strains together that already existed in the Hebrew Scripture and makes a profound synthesis that places *love* at the center of life. It is not that these ideas were new. He just saw this profound shift in emphasis as the core of the Jewish faith.

We also see the same kind of thinking at work in the continuation of the Sermon on the Mount in which Jesus teaches:

> So whatever you wish that men would do to you, do so to them; for this is the law and the prophets. (Matt 7:12)

This is commonly known as the Golden Rule and is probably seen by Jesus as simply a different form of the second part of his summary of the law above. What is particularly compelling here is to notice that in each case there is a self-reference. The difficulty arises from the fact that if you have trouble loving yourself, you will have trouble loving your neighbor. If you have low expectations regarding what you would have others do to you, you will have low expectations regarding how you treat others. This self-reference is particularly problematic for the mafia or for those addicted to sadomasochism. In fact, they probably assume that they operate according to this guideline. When the mafia is about to dispatch a particularly troublesome member of an opposing crime family, they remind the poor soul that "this is just business," at which the forlorn dispatchee acknowledges that there are no hard feelings—it is just business. When sadomasochists whip and beat each other with glee, they are reflecting a mutual agreement to "treat each other as they would like to be treated." For us in our daily lives, we seem to be perfectly comfortable being ignored or treated with indifference because we treat others the same way. If someone fails to meet us at a previously arranged time and place, all too often we shrug it off without being hurt or offended, because we have such low expectations of ourselves and of others. Jesus must have seen the dilemma. The existing commandments could take you only so far. He cracks the problem wide open by offering a *new commandment*. It is no longer enough to love our neighbor as ourselves. We are called to love our neighbor as Jesus loved us—and that is how God loves us. The self-reference is replaced with a God-reference. And by the way, he does not do this in response to the questioning of the Pharisees or as an extension of his regular teaching ministry—he does this at the Last Supper when he is spending his last hours alive teaching the apostles the deepest pearls of truth before his arrest and execution.

For Jesus to have phrased this teaching in this way must have meant that he intended for it to be of paramount importance. A Jew would not have dreamed up a *new com-mandment* lightly. All of his life had been centered on the Commandments. He knew better than anyone the central place they held in the life of the Jewish community, and yet he is adding one—what I am calling *the eleventh*:[20]

---

20 From a purely scholarly point of view, some might argue that the term "commandments" should be more broadly interpreted, and certainly the case could be made. Clearly in the Old Testament the term is applied more broadly than the ten "words" received by Moses on Mt. Sinai. In the Gospels (NRSV), however, there are only 10 uses of the word "command-ments," and each uses the Greek word *entolon* (or a variation).

1. Whoever then relaxes one of the least of these commandments . . . (Matt 5:19)
2. . . . to enter into life, keep the commandments . . . (Matt 19:17)
3. On these two commandments hang all the law and the prophets. (Matt 22:40)
4. You know the commandments: 'Do not kill, Do not commit adultery, Do not steal . . . (6 of 10) (Mark 10:19)
5. And they were both righteous before God, walking in all the com-mandments and ordinances of the Lord blamelessly. (Luke 1:6)
6. You know the commandments: 'Do not commit adultery . . . (5 of 10) (Luke 18:20)
7. If you love me you will keep my commandments. (John 14:15)
8. They who have my commandments and keep them . . . (John 14:21).
9. If you keep my commandments, you will . . . (John 15:10)
10. As I have kept my father's commandments . . . (John 15:10)

Clearly both the authors of the Gospels and Jesus himself use the word in different senses pointing toward the Decalogue in two instances as well as in a more general sense of either "all the commandments and ordinances of the Lord" or "all the things that I have told you." It seems that if Jesus is adding just one more "thing" he would have just told them to love one another as he had loved them. By saying "I give you a new commandment," he is setting this above all the other things he has "commanded them." One could at least make the case that he, by using the word "new," intended this to sit at the level of the other Decalogue (Ten Words) commandments that seem—even from a Hebrew perspective—to have taken a place of precedence over all the other ordinances and commandments (613—*mitz-vot*). To be safe I could have used the title *The Six-hundred and Fourteenth*

. . . that you love one another even as I have loved
you. (John 13:34)

By this he changes the entire perspective. From then on
he becomes the yardstick for our behavior to one another and
love becomes the medium of exchange—the *lingua franca*—for
all Christian communities of faith. Not just any love—but the
love of Christ. From this we can assume that an important task
is to see how his love acted and influenced the lives of those
around him. But he does not stop there. He must leave no
doubt concerning the place that his love is to occupy among
his followers. He goes on to say:

By this all men will know that you are my disciples, if you have love for one another. (John 13:35)

In other words, we are to be marked as followers of Jesus
not by the number of times we go to church or the amount of
money we give to our parish or by the stature we attain in our
church hierarchy—but by our love for one another. It is this
clear directive that forces us to look ever so carefully at the
way we operate in our respective congregations and how we
relate to others outside those congregations.

Now you might say that we really don't need a new commandment. If we love God completely, then we will love ourselves completely, and that the complete love of God becomes
the yardstick by which we love our neighbor. But what does
the complete love of God look like? We could start by seeing
how God loves us. The problem arises from the fact that there

---

Commandment, but that seemed a bit clumsy, obscure, and not very compelling. With what I hope is a reasonable understanding of the scholarly challenges, I have chosen to err on the side of simplicity and emphasis.

is a bit of a disconnect between our love of God and God's love for us. Without a clear understanding of how God loves us, we do not really know how to love God, let alone ourselves and our neighbor. Jesus, of course, fills in the blank by showing us how God loves us:

> I in them and thou in me, that they may become perfectly one, so that the world may know that thou hast sent me and hast loved them even as thou hast loved me. (John 17:23)

> As the Father has loved me, so have I loved you; abide in my love. (John 15:9)

The Father loves both the Son and the rest of us. The Son loves us in the same way in which he is loved by the Father. So now when Jesus shows us his own love, he is showing us the love of the Father. When he then tells us to love one another as he has loved us, he is telling us to love one another as God loves us. We are then called to love God with all our heart, soul, and mind. In fact, we are called to love God as we are loved *by* God through Christ. The circle is complete. If you think what I am calling the *Eleventh Commandment* is no big deal, take it up with *him*. I didn't say it was a *new commandment*—he did. He must have thought it was a big deal, and it behooves us to take him at his word.

If we do this, the *Eleventh Commandment* becomes our guiding light, and we have no choice but to plumb its deepest implications to understand how it is to be manifest in the community of faith. What follows is an exploration of this precise focus.

11

THE LOVE OF CHRIST

Our first objective is to look carefully at the love of Christ. What does this kind of love look like? How is this love different from our normal understanding of love? Since there are many ways in which we use the word "love," we might need to do some clarifying. The uses of the word may include loving golf, loving my parents, loving my dog, loving my rose bushes, loving my next door neighbor, loving my spouse, loving those who have sacrificed their lives for me that I might be free, loving the poor and destitute, loving my enemy, loving my Lord and savior Jesus Christ, and loving God with all my heart, strength, soul, and mind. In other words, we use the word "love" to refer to a very wide range of situations, and clearly we don't mean the same thing when we use the same word in these very different ways. Our challenge here is to understand enough of these different ways of loving so that we can begin to characterize and distinguish the love of Christ. Although the process of defining love is certainly not something new, it is an essential starting point for our discussion.

I myself began with C. S. Lewis's *The Four Loves*[21] as a foundation, and I recommend it highly.

EROS

If I say, "I love raspberry ice cream," this is probably the most superficial application of the word. It simply means that it stimulates my senses in a very positive way. I get a lot of enjoyment out of it. To say that I love the Denver Broncos football team means that I have developed a personal stake in their activities. I have tied my own well-being to theirs. If they win, I feel good. If they lose, I feel depressed. (Oh, for a redo of Super Bowl XLVIII!) We could extend this kind of self-serving love to include any one-sided relationship that exists only for the purpose of self-gratification. Availing oneself of prostitution would certainly fall into this category, as well as some unhealthy marriages that function to the mutual self-gratification of the spouses. This kind of love depends solely on the level of gratification experienced. Lewis calls this the most basic kind of "need love". When this gratification falls below some level or threshold, the reason for the relationship ceases—and so does the "love." This kind of self-serving love might be called *eros* or erotic love.

But that is not the whole story of *eros*. Here is a bit of Pope Benedict's first encyclical entitled *Deus Caritas Est* (God is love—December 25, 2005).[22]

---

21 C. S. Lewis, *Surprised by Joy* and *The Four Loves* (New York: Houghton Mifflin Harcourt, 2011).

22 Benedict XVI, *Deus Caritas Est* [Encyclical Letter on Christian Love], accessed September 17, 2009, http://www.vatican.va/holy_father/benedict_xvi/encyclicals/documents/hf_ben-xvi_enc_20051225_deus-caritas-est_en.html.

Evidently, *eros* needs to be disciplined and puri-
fied if it is to provide not just fleeting pleasure,
but a certain foretaste of the pinnacle of our existence, of that beatitude for which our whole being yearns. (Paragraph 4)

Yet it is neither the spirit alone nor the body
alone that loves: it is man, the person, a unified
creature composed of body and soul, who loves.
Only when both dimensions are truly united,
does man attain his full stature. Only thus is
love—*eros*—able to mature and attain its authentic grandeur. (Paragraph 5)

There's a *grandeur* to *eros*? Is there important territory between the self-serving interpretation of *eros* and the completely self-giving interpretation of the love of God? The
Pope boldly describes this territory as the grandeur of *eros*. It
is the territory of union. This union may involve psychological union, physical union, or both.[23] But I will simply state
without attribution that the highest form of intimate physical
love is the union of differences. A union that requires openness not just to points of familiarity and likeness—as two
human beings with common needs, aspirations and interests—but also openness to the profound differences that mutually inform our own existence—a union of differences that
completes a whole that is greater than the sum of the parts.
If you feel an overpowering urge to be one with another,
the closest we can come is in the exposed and vulnerable

---

[23] Now this becomes a bit tricky for an author, because the first question
that comes to mind might be, "How do you know?" And my answer is,
"I'm not telling."

physical and psychological intimacy we call "making love." It is not simply self-serving *sex* (Lewis calls this *Venus*), but the highest form of *eros* that results in a profound union of body and soul, the material and the spiritual. It is this *erotic* union that the mystics have referred to as the highest form of union with God. This is not an ecstasy of *self*—but an ecstasy of *union*. Thus, there is a continuum of *eros* from a self-centered gratification to a more mutually self-giving, other-receiving union that leads one right to the threshold of a *total* self-giving and other-receiving act that is the kind of love God has for us, and we are called to have for God.

PHILIA

To say that I love my sister, Penny, can take me in another direction. I might mean that the deep filial bond that surrounds our common family and history makes her an important part of my life. Her very existence is intimately related to my existence, and I experience a sense of value and a particular affinity toward her. When she recalls something of our shared childhood, it is as if I were able to touch not only a precious shared object, but also something that transcends both of us in our union with our parents. This kind of love is what philosophers would call *philia*. This is a kind of conditional love that derives its force from the continuing mutually-rewarding relationship. This kind of love also shows up in friendships and marriages. Unfortunately, it can be broken as soon as the relationship is broken. One of the saddest fractures is between members of a family as a result of a misunderstanding or a real disagreement of values. All the priceless connections are tossed out the window, and their lives are all the poorer for the loss.

But again, *philia* has much deeper possibilities. C. S. Lewis delves deeply into the realm of friendship. Here we find connections that are not circumstances of birth or location, but are recognized and chosen. Friendship is based on some form of common interest or goal, but we are not talking about acquaintances here. We may have acquaintances that center on a number of different activities. I have rowing "friends," church "friends," ballet "friends" (for goodness sakes don't tell anyone), chorus "friends," and so on, but the kinds of friends we are really concerned with here are those that transcend specifics. They may have started under the umbrella of a specific shared interest, but eventually they evolved to an entirely different level. This level is based on an ability to communicate because of shared vocabulary tied to a shared set of values or a shared set of experiences. From this ability to communicate comes a *desire* to communicate that is followed by a transparency that both leads to and depends on a shared trust. Now we are getting somewhere—*trust*. A friend you can trust with all your foibles, frustrations, idiosyncrasies, joys, raging faults, and heartaches is rare indeed.

Lewis talks about the rarity of this kind of friendship in modern literature. Recently, I was watching an old episode of *Route 66* with Marty Milner (playing Tod Stiles) and George Maharis (playing Buzz Murdock). At one point they are walking into their motel, and Buzz puts his arm over Tod's shoulder. Now we are not talking about homosexuality but friendship—the kind of friendship that is represented by the biblical persons of David and Jonathan (no relation). This kind of friendship is deep, abiding, and unconditional. It is the kind of relationship that is not demanding. True friends may go for months or years without communicating, but when they do, they simply pick up where they left off.

You really need to read Lewis on this one, but let me recall some of his images. These kinds of friends are not found
gazing yearningly into each other's eyes as lovers do, but
are found gazing ahead in the same direction as if viewing
some common journey or goal. These kinds of friends do
not talk about their relationship as lovers do, but talk about
everything else.[24] This kind of friendship is not about what
it *brings*, but what it *is*. It is much more about *being* than *doing*—although doing certainly can be an important part of it.

The sense we get is that true friendship is at some level
spiritual. In fact, there is a classic work on spiritual friendship
by Aelred of Rievaulx that addresses this very issue.[25] Here
we see the depth of relationship that is possible in friendship.
It is also interesting to note what Jesus says to his apostles:

> This is my commandment, that you love one an-
> other as I have loved you. Greater love has no
> man than this, that a man lay down his life for
> his friends. You are my friends if you do what I
> command you. No longer do I call you servants,
> for the servant does not know what his master is
> doing; but I have called you friends, for all that I
> have heard from my Father I have made known
> to you. You did not choose me, but I chose you
> and appointed you that you should go and bear
> fruit and that your fruit should abide; so that
> whatever you ask the Father in my name, he may
> give it to you. This I command you, to love one
> another. (John 15:12–17)

---

24 C. S. Lewis, *Surprised by Joy* and *The Four Loves*, 265.
25 Aelred of Rievaulx, *Spiritual Friendship* (trans. Lawrence C. Braceland;
Trappist, KY: Cistercian Publications, 2010).

This linkage between friendship and love is most clear in this passage. The Greek word that is being translated as "friend" is the word *philia*, and yet he clearly is pointing toward a depth that transcends our own use of the word "friend." Here friends are those for whom one would be willing to die. We see this in extraordinarily dangerous situations in which some have literally given up their lives that others might live. Stories of soldiers throwing themselves on a hand grenade to save their comrades evoke this idea. Parents dying to save their children from a fire and strangers helping strangers in the midst of a devastating storm like Hurricanes Katrina and Sandy, the over 400 first responders at the World Trade Center tragedy who perished trying to save others, the ten volunteer firemen in West, Texas who died trying to keep the fertilizer plant from exploding, the fifty Ukrainian emergency workers who died of acute radiation poisoning as a result of their efforts to halt the meltdown of the nuclear reactor at Chernobyl—all these bring to mind this kind of selfless sacrifice. Specifically Jesus' friends are those for whom the Son of God is willing to lay down his own precious life—a life that is defined *by* and *as* the eternal life of God.

Here also friends are those who do what he commanded. Now, this can't mean that friends are simply those who do what we want them to do. He must be meaning that friends are those who are on the path of truth and love that can only be laid out by the Son of God. In this same vein, Jesus established his relationship to the apostles as that of friendship rather than of servant-hood, because he gave them all that had been given to him. In other words, friends are those who share the most intimate aspects of their lives with each other—they share their very *being*. They are friends because they know and understand what each other is doing and why. This is another way of saying that through this kind of deep friendship, Jesus has offered them all that he was. This kind of transparency and selfless giving is a hallmark of the kind of spiritual friendship we will be talking about as we develop our ideas of a true community of faith.

We also see the idea that friendship is based on some form of choice. While other forms of love are based on factors that are to some extent beyond our control—our appetites, our instincts, or our circumstances—friendship is based on a choice—a decision to enter into a deeper relationship with someone else. As such, it depends on a willingness to invest our time and energy in the development of that friendship. It requires a commitment. Love-at-first-sight or at least at-first-encounter has much in common with *eros*. *Philia*, however, requires something more—a desire and willingness to go deeper. For this reason, there are precious friendships that never get developed because one or the other party was either not paying enough attention to recognize the opportunity or was too busy to invest in it. While *philia* inherently arises among siblings, its depth must also be developed. At other times, there are deep friendships that develop from the most mundane circumstances, ones that throw two unlikely persons into a situation, forcing them to shed the mask and take the time to see the true common ground of friendship. Those in prison camps during war often experience this kind of friendship. Those in mission work in a strange country can be thrown together for long periods of time during which they must learn to relate at a deeper level than those of us who function in our own little isolated worlds. Any soldier in a fox hole can develop this kind of indelible bond with others in the same hole, "praying" for reinforcements or struggling for survival or being cold or wet or exhausted or otherwise just being miserable—together. Circumstances alone will not form friendships, but they can certainly be the catalyst.

Finally, we see that true friendships are fruitful. This aspect of friendship is not so obvious. One way to get at the depth of this concept is to recognize a wide range of potential fruits of any relationship. We might start with the idea that friendships result in some form of ministry. This is certainly not always the case, but we could assert that true friendship involves a kind of natural generosity to each other. This is ministry in its most basic form. We might also think that friendships are creative and offer the possibility of developing something new. This is probably closer to the kind of fruit we are talking about. There are really only two choices here: either a relationship is self-serving and as such tends to be conservative in nature and therefore not creative, or it is other-serving and by its very nature leads to the growth of ourselves and others and therefore *is* creative. In other words, growth and change are fruitful and therefore, by definition, creative. Something new is evolving. Something old is not simply being conserved. The fruits of a true friendship have to do with its openness, honesty, and transparency. True friends don't just talk *at* each other, changing the subject as a new thought pops into each other's head. True friends listen carefully to each other. They look for points of contact, acknowledge points of variance, use as a springboard points of agreement and relish the *process* of creating something brand new out of the materials that were brought to the table by each other. If the relationship is not creative—if neither party delights in learning something new from the interaction—the chances are very good that, by definition, the relationship is too shallow to be termed a deep friendship.

STORGE

A third kind of love is captured by the word "affection," denoted by the Greek word *storge*. This is the kind of love that parents have for their children. Its most notable quality is that it is not dependent upon a passion for fulfillment like *eros* or on some commonality of purpose or pathway like the deepest form of *philia*. As Lewis says, it is the humblest form of love. It can exist between those who have nothing identifiable in common except for the fact that they are here—together. It has none of the flash of *eros* or the depth of *philia*, but grows steadily as circumstances demand. In fact, this is a case where circumstances alone are enough. It always takes time to develop because it depends on a growing appreciation of the qualities of the other that may be deeply imbedded in their characters. Affection can occur between dog and cat, baron and gardener, and diva and maid. Recall the movie *Driving Miss Daisy* with Jessica Tandy and Morgan Freeman.[26] It is a perfect rendering of the kind of disparate personalities and social statuses that can exhibit remarkable affection. Affection knows no natural boundaries other than the time it takes for steadfastness to surface. It is this constancy that seems to underlie affection. It apparently cannot develop under inconsistent, hit-or-miss circumstances. As Lewis says, it is often noted by the term "old," such as in the phrases "good old Fred" or "she is as comfortable as an old pair of slippers."[27]

One of the more interesting encounters I have had recently came when I had lunch with a professor from my master's degree program in the Geology Department at the University of South Carolina. During our conversation, I began to get the sense that I was not everything he wanted me to be.

26 Warner Brothers, 1989.
27 C. S. Lewis, *Surprised by Joy* and *The Four Loves*, 243.

I think it had something to do with a feeling that I needed a bit more humility (which may in fact be true) and that our relationship was strained because of it. I asked him to lunch because he was important to me, but when I shared with him this observation, he responded that I should not "kid a kidder." In other words, he could see through my evident insincerity. For my part, I thought I was being perfectly sincere and offering an important gesture of affection toward him. His rejection of that gesture was both painful and bewildering. After I staggered away from this disastrous encounter, I spent considerable time trying to figure out the nature of our disconnection. Clearly, he was operating on an entirely different wavelength than I was. I was ready to bask in our friendship, and he was crouching ready to attack as a result of a long-held grudge of some sort. Here is my conclusion. The people who are (or should be) valuable to us are the people who were *there* as we were being formed. They are not necessarily those who were nicest to us or who taught us some profound truth that changed our lives for the better. They are not necessarily those we loved most or were best friends with. The people most valuable to us are the ones who were present and in some meaningful way participated in our growth. My professor clearly fell into this category of folks who were and continue to be important to me—and I love them for that. Stew Hollingsworth, Jack Moore, and Don Millenbruch from Union Carbide were there. Mrs. Bobo and Mr. Slaughter from high school; Jim Lowe, Felder Dorn, and David Camp from Sewanee; John Carpenter, Dave and Marge Hanselman, and Bob Gardner at the University of South Carolina; and Derrill Kerrick, Bill Vogely, and John Tilton from Penn State were there, too. The women I have dated have had a profound influence on me, even if many would have liked to strangle me. The relationships between men and women can be nothing less than life altering as they cut to the core of who we are as human beings. I could go on and on, but my point is that this feeling is not just an intellectual appreciation—but a true love. They are an indelible part of me that no amount of soap can ever wash off. I am who, to some extent, they made me. This affection is really quite different from *eros* and *philia*, but is a no less real and no less powerful form of love.

Affection, or *storge*, also has one important quality—out of it can evolve *eros* or *philia*. Out of an appreciation of the unique characteristics of another to whom we might not initially be attracted by passionate or brotherly love may gradually grow a deeper relationship that could evolve into other forms of love. The converse can also be true, out of *eros* and *philia* can evolve true affection. While *eros* and *philia* do not in and of themselves necessitate a deep appreciation of characteristics that might be somewhat alien, such an appreciation certainly should grow as one engages in other forms of love. In fact, affection is closely related to the idea of compassion. It was Jesus' ability to see deeply into the center of one's being and to recognize one's woundedness that gave him a constant sense of compassion for all those he encountered. While for some it often takes a considerable period of time to develop this kind of affection and compassion, he seemed to live in a place where these forms of love were constantly operative.[28]

Now that we are equipped with the images of unitive *eros*,

---

28 One of the most remarkable aspects of *The Four Loves* is Lewis's ability to identify traps associated with each kind of love. How can the depth and wonder of *eros, philia*, and *storge* be turned into demons that can destroy us? While it far beyond the scope of our purpose here, I would highly recommend it to the reader.

the commonality of purpose found in *philia*, and the compassion of *storge*, we can begin to appreciate the kind of love that God has for us. In Hebrew, this is called *hesed*, or steadfast love. In Greek, the word would be *agape*, or unconditional love. Often it is translated as *charity*. This kind of love is a free gift and has no strings attached. It too is based on a relationship, but one that cannot be broken. The *affect* can be broken if the object of the love walks away, but the one who gives the love never ceases to offer it. The way Jesus loved is the way God loves, so if we want to know how God loves, we should look at Jesus, and if we want to know how we are to love—you guessed it—we should look at Jesus. How did he love and how did he teach others to love? Consider the following:

> Greater love has no man than this, that a man lay down his life for his friends. (John 15:13)

> But I say to you, Love your enemies and pray for those who persecute you . . . (Matt 5:44)

> Then turning toward the woman he said to Simon: Do you see this woman? I entered your house, you gave me no water for my feet, but she has wet my feet with her tears and wiped them with her hair. You gave me no kiss, but from the time I came in she has not ceased to kiss my feet. You did not anoint my head with oil, but she has anointed my feet with ointment. Therefore I tell you, her sins, which are many, are forgiven, for she loved much; but he who is forgiven little, loves little. (Luke 7:44–48)

When the Son of man comes in his glory, and all the angels with him, then he will sit on his glorious throne. Before him will be gathered all the nations, and he will separate them one from another as a shepherd separates the sheep from the goats, and he will place the sheep at his right hand, but the goats at the left. Then the King will say to those at his right hand, "Come, O blessed of my Father, inherit the kingdom prepared for you from the foundation of the world; for I was hungry and you gave me food, I was thirsty and you gave me drink, I was a stranger and you welcomed me, I was naked and you clothed me, I was sick and you visited me, I was in prison and you came to me." Then the righteous will answer him, "Lord, when did we see thee hungry and feed thee, or thirsty and give thee drink? And when did we see thee a stranger and welcome thee, or naked and clothe thee? And when did we see thee sick or in prison and visit thee?" And the King will answer them, "Truly, I say to you, as you did it to one of the least of these my brethren, you did it to me." (Matt 25:31–40)

These and many more statements, concerning how Jesus treated people and how he expected his followers to treat others, say something important about the way that Jesus loved. He was full of mercy and compassion. Somehow he was able to look beneath the surface and see our woundedness. He was able to be generous and kind even when others were ungenerous and unkind to him. He was able to get his ego out of the way and think only about others. He did not allow their negative response to him to have any influence over his response to them. When we look at Jesus, we get a picture of love that is gentle, kind, thoughtful, and compassionate. But then we get statements like the following:

> Woe to you, scribes and Pharisees, hypocrites! for you are like whitewashed tombs, which outwardly appear beautiful, but within they are full of dead men's bones and all uncleanness. (Matt 23:27)

> And Jesus entered the temple of God and drove out all who sold and bought in the temple, and he overturned the tables of the money-changers and the seats of those who sold pigeons. (Matt 21:12)

Is this also love? Did Jesus love the Pharisees and the money-changers? He loved them enough to tell them the truth. We are often repelled from such love for fear of criticism and rejection. Where do we see love acted out in this way? One place is in the radical interventions held by family and friends for one who is enslaved to recalcitrant addiction. Sometimes the only way out of this kind of trap is for those who love us to step in, grab us by the scruff of the neck and give us a good yank. There is no question that the one held by addiction will not respond favorably to our "tough love," until long after the fact when he or she realizes that it was only through that intervention that the back of the addictive force was broken.

In other words, the nature of true love is not always easy to discern. It does not always look nice and soft and fluffy, but it *is* always grounded in care for others and a desire for the truth. As we said, love without truth is a sham and truth without love is cruelty. When Jesus says, ". . . and you will know the truth, and the truth will make you free" (John 8:32), he is placing a high premium on the truth—not only the truth about himself but *all* truth. To the degree that we are bearers of that truth—any truth—as best we can, we could say that we are bearers of the love of Christ.

It is this kind of love that God offers us, it is this kind of love that Jesus showed to us, and it is this kind of love that he holds up as the pattern for our relationships as Christians and as members of the Body of Christ. It has qualities of deep friendship in that it requires a choice and results in a high level of transparency and self-giving. It involves growth and change and therefore is creative by its very nature. And it has the qualities of *eros* in that it is highly unitive, desiring a level of oneness that is reflected in the relationship between the Son and the Father. To understand the depth of this kind of oneness, we need to explore the relationship between the Father, the Son, and the Holy Spirit. In other words, we need to have a basic understanding of the Trinity if we are to grasp the depth of the love Jesus Christ has for us—and expects us to have for one another.

12

THE TRINITY

The God who revealed himself in the Old Testament as YHWH is in the New Testament more fully revealed as *one in three persons.* This idea that the one God can have this triune character has been a puzzlement to the Church from the very beginning of its reflection on the Christ event. And yet the activity of the three persons—Father, Son and Holy Spirit—has been unequivocally clear—*I mean crystal clear*— from Scripture. Consider Paul's statements:

> But when the time had fully come, *God sent forth his Son,* born of woman, born under the law, to redeem those who were under the law, so that we might receive adoption as sons. And because you are sons, *God has sent the Spirit* of his Son into our hearts, crying, "Abba! *Father!*" So through God you are no longer a slave but a son, and if a son then an heir. (Gal 4:4–7)

Here we see just one of many instances in which Father,

Son and Holy Spirit (my emphasis above) are shown to be
central to the Christian understanding of the entire Christ
event—and therefore central to all of salvation history. We
also see that in just a few sentences we have encountered the
two broad ways in which the Church has addressed the reality and the meaning of the Trinity. The first is the Trinity
as it is revealed in history and expressed in the Gospels. We
call this the *economic* Trinity, because it is expressed in the
exchange between God and humanity in historic time. The
second is the Trinity as it is understood *in itself* and revealed
through the deliberations of the Church on the economic
Trinity. We call this the *immanent* Trinity. In other words,
we arrive at our understanding of the immanent Trinity (one
God in three Persons) by contemplating the economic Trinity (the Son of God came from the Father to save humanity
and sent us the Holy Spirit to guide us in our journey back
to oneness with the Father). Therefore, our understanding of
the Trinity in itself is grounded in our understanding of how
the Father, Son and Holy Spirit are revealed in salvation history. These two vantage points cannot be separated.

We might go a bit further and fill out how the economic and immanent Trinities are distinguished. The former is
founded on the *missions* of the three persons as reflected in
the Gospels and the latter is founded on the way in which
the three persons came to be—we call this the *processions*.
The missions relate to the role of the Father as Creator, the
Son as Savior and the Holy Spirit as Sanctifier. The processions relate to the very careful way in which the Church has
expressed how the Father is *uncreated*, the Son is *begotten* of
the Father, and Holy Spirit *proceeds* from the Father and the
Son. The rest of this chapter fills out some of these ideas and
addresses their meaning regarding the community of faith.

While we read about the activity of Father, Son and Holy Spirit, there is little question that most Christians are unclear how an understanding of the Trinity informs their lives. Consequently, most Christians are functional "Monarchians." That is to say, they are not only monotheists (one God, which is a good thing), but they function as if God is only one and not *three in one*. Likewise, the Church as a whole has historically struggled to articulate clearly not only what the Trinity is *in itself*, but also what it *means* to us as followers of Jesus Christ. The Church Fathers as well as theologians through the centuries have tried many different ways and have used many different metaphors to try to get at what is universally acknowledged as the central mystery of faith. Because the idea of community—particularly the idea of the community of faith—is squarely grounded on our understanding of the love of Christ, which in turn is squarely grounded on our understanding of the love of God as reflected in the relations among the Father, Son, and Holy Spirit, some form of elucidation of the mystery of the Trinity is important to us. If we can understand both who God is *in himself* and how he has *functioned* in salvation history, we will have a firmer foundation on which to build our understanding of the Kingdom of God on earth as reflected in the Christian community of faith.

Because this is such a convoluted subject, perhaps we should start at the beginning with some sort of attempt to articulate the basics of Trinitarian theology. This is probably a ridiculous task for one who is clearly not a theologian, but just maybe we might be able to say something of value that will set up our later discussion of the community of faith. First, we might want to make a distinction between the Scriptural sources of our understanding of the Trinity and

our understanding of the nature of the Trinity we have derived from theological contemplation. It should be appreciated that the need for any understanding at all comes foremost
from the fact of the Incarnation of Jesus Christ as the Son of
God. If we had had no Son, we would not have needed to
struggle with his relationship to the Father. So we can state
unequivocally that, while there are wonderful and insightful
allusions to person-like "others" in the Hebrew Bible, they
would not compel us toward an elucidation of a triune God
in their own regard without the Incarnation.

What we learn from the Incarnation is that the man Jesus
of Nazareth was, and is believed by Christians to have been,
sent by the Father for the salvation of the world—to return
the world to right relationship to himself. The question that
Christ asked of his followers when he was in his earthly ministry, and of us now, is, "Who do you say that I am?" Recall Peter's response—"You are the Christ, the Son of the
living God" (Matt 16:16). More importantly, Jesus' reply is
most telling—"Blessed are you, Simon Bar-Jona! For flesh
and blood has not revealed this to you, but my Father who
is in heaven" (Matt 16:17). In other words, our understanding of Jesus' sonship—and just exactly what that entails—is a
statement of faith. We get hints of the depth of the relationship throughout the Gospels by Jesus' own words, his works,
as well as the words of the Gospel writers, but it is still a mystery accessible only by faith. The most stunning statement is
from the opening words of the Gospel of John:

> In the beginning was the Word, and the Word
> was with God, and the Word was God. He was
> in the beginning with God; all things were made
> through him, and without him was not anything

made that was made. In him was life, and the life was the light of men. The light shines in the darkness, and the darkness has not overcome it.

There was a man sent from God, whose name was John. He came for testimony, to bear witness to the light, that all might believe through him. He was not the light, but came to bear witness to the light.

The true light that enlightens every man was coming into the world. He was in the world, and the world was made through him, yet the world knew him not. He came to his own home, and his own people received him not. But to all who received him, who believed in his name, he gave power to become children of God; who were born, not of blood nor of the will of the flesh nor of the will of man, but of God.

And the Word became flesh and dwelt among us, full of grace and truth; we have beheld his glory, glory as of the only-begotten Son from the Father. (John 1:1–14)

There is no question that the writer of the Gospel intends for us to appreciate an eternal relationship between the Son and the Father. The challenge of the early Church was to dispel confusion and establish an understanding of this eternal relationship that preserved the validity of the salvation event. From this and other statements in the New Testament, the Church developed its understanding of the intimate relationship of the Son to the Father. The Father begets the Son who is given the full divine status of the Father. In other words, the Father gives the Son all that the Father is—he holds nothing back or reserves nothing for himself. This complete gift of self is important in our understanding of the love of Christ. Not only does the Father give all of himself to the Son, but he also begets the Son in such a way that the union of Father and Son is total. Now, this is where analogies run a bit dry on us. The best we might be able to do is to think of the union of a man and a woman whose passion for total oneness draws them into the most intimate physical and psychological union. But they are still limited by the physicality of their bodies. As much as they might desire to be totally in union with one another down to the molecular level, they simply cannot. It is said that angels, because of their non-corporeal nature can, in fact, experience a unitive love that does involve a total absorption (for lack of a better word). Now we stretch to carry that union to an even higher level, and all we are left with is a pointer. We have no words or concepts that adequately describe this union of Father and Son, but we know that it is more complete than anything we can imagine. We can say what it is *not*, but we have great difficulty saying what it *is*. We do, however, understand the effects to some extent. St. Maximus the Confessor would say, "The whole Divinity is in the whole Father and the whole Father is in the whole Divinity. The whole Divinity is in the whole Son and the whole Son is in the whole Divinity."[29] If you "do the math," it sounds like the Son and Father must be the same entity, but there are two "persons" that have distinct identities defined by the fact that the Son is:

---

29 G. E. H. Palmer, et. al., ed., *The Philokalia* (Winchester, Massachusetts: Faber and Faber, 1986), 137.

. . . the Only Begotten Son of God, born of the
Father before all ages. God from God, Light from
Light, true God from true God, begotten, not
made, consubstantial with the Father; through
him all things were made. For us men and for
our salvation he came down from heaven . . .[30]

In other words, the Son is the one identical "essence"
as the Father, but is still a distinct "person" who can come
down from heaven independently of the Father, and yet is
perfectly "one" with the Father. Here is a little (and entirely
inadequate) thought exercise. Imagine a Venn diagram (two
circles representing two sets of things) that represents the
divine characteristics of the Father and the Son that over-
laps a little. In other words, in this picture they share *some*
characteristics.

Father 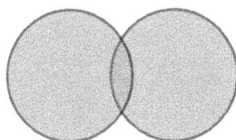 Son

Now move the circles over one another until all of the
divine characteristics of the Father are also the divine characteristics of the Son.

Father 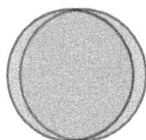 Son

Now it starts to look like both sets are the same. Now
imagine that each member of each set has a subtle marker,

30 Nicene Creed from the new Catholic Missal translation.

such that while it may look the same as a corresponding member of the other set, it is recognizably different simply because of where it came from—those of the Father are *uncreated* and those of the Son are eternally *begotten*. Well, as I said, it is a mystery that we can dance around and never get to—a reality that is known only by God.

But what about the Holy Spirit? The descriptions of the Holy Spirit are a bit more subtle. When Jesus says, "Go therefore and make disciples of all nations, baptizing them in the name of the Father and of the Son and of the Holy Spirit" (Matt 28:19), he clearly is placing the Father, Son, and Holy Spirit on the same plane. When he said, "But the Counselor, the Holy Spirit, whom the Father will send in my name, he will teach you all things, and bring to your remembrance all that I have said to you" (John 14:26), he gives the Holy Spirit exalted status as an integral part of salvation history and the activity of God in the life of humanity. The way we express this is by saying that the Holy Spirit *proceeds* from both the Father and the Son. This *proceeding* is precisely the one characteristic that differentiates the Holy Spirit from the Father and the Son.[31] Some have tried to capture the differences by saying that the Father is the Creator, the Son is the Redeemer, and the Holy Spirit is the Sanctifier, which is sort of true according to their *missions*—as long as we don't limit each one to these mutually exclusive characteristics and end up with three different gods. Again, St. Maximus would admonish us that everything that is in the Son and Father is in the Holy Spirit, and everything that is in the Holy Spirit is

---

31 The Eastern Orthodox would assert that the original creed stated that the Holy Spirit proceeds from the Father only. This difference was a major sticking point, and one of the causes of the great split of the eastern from the western Church in 1054 AD.

in the Father and the Son. In other words, when we are confronted by the Son, we are confronted equally by the Father and the Holy Spirit. If we are careful, we can say that we have access *to* the Father *through* the Son *in* the Holy Spirit. This is one ancient formula that seems to be very helpful. Again, we can think of adding another circle to our Venn diagram and then merging it with the other two. Now we have three distinct "somethings" that we call *persons*—each with all the properties of the others and yet each one has a different origin and *tends* to play a different role in salvation history.

It was up to the Church in sequential councils, in response to a series of theological challenges that threatened to undermine the power and finality of the Incarnation, to develop doctrine that established unequivocally several essential concepts about the nature of God:

1. The God of Jesus Christ is the same God of Abraham, Isaac, and Jacob. The monotheistic theology of the Hebrew Bible must be kept intact. There is one God.

2. There are three "somethings" that form an integral part of the Godhead, known in salvation history as the Father, Son, and Holy Spirit, whose relationship to one another form the unique foundation of the Christian faith. This is the Trinity.

3. The Church eventually arrived at the term *persons* to describe the three, but it must be understood that the definition of the term as

it is used here is specifically established only in the context of the nature of the Trinity.

4. The three "persons" played different roles in salvation history, but could not be seen as differentiated by those roles, lest we be left with three distinct gods.

5. The equal status of each of the three *persons* must be preserved by asserting that they are *consubstantial* or have the same divine *nature*. In other words, there is no subordination within the Trinity of three persons.

6. The statement that "God is love" (1 John 4:8) is central to this relationship, not just because God loves us, but more especially because God is love *in himself* through the very essence of the Holy Trinity.

Let's first look at this status thing. To do this we should look again at the creedal statement developed at the Council of Nicaea (AD 325) and refined at the Council of Constantinople (AD 381):

I believe in one God, the Father almighty, maker of heaven and earth, of all things visible and invisible.

I believe in one Lord Jesus Christ, the Only Begotten Son of God, born of the Father before all ages. God from God, Light from Light, true God

from true God, begotten, not made, consubstantial with the Father; through him all things were
made. For us men and for our salvation he came
down from heaven, and by the Holy Spirit was
incarnate of the Virgin Mary, and became man.
For our sake he was crucified under Pontius Pilate, he suffered death and was buried, and rose
again on the third day in accordance with the
Scriptures. He ascended into heaven and is seated at the right hand of the Father. He will come
again in glory to judge the living and the dead
and his kingdom will have no end.

I believe in the Holy Spirit, the Lord, the giver of
life, who proceeds from the Father and the Son,
who with the Father and the Son is adored and
glorified, who has spoken through the prophets.[32]

The major effort here was to assure that the Father, Son,
and Holy Spirit were established with equal status in the
Godhead, the distinctions being captured in the words *begotten* and *proceeding*. At this point, we are still not so much
concerned with the structure of the Trinity itself as we are in
establishing that there are three "somethings" that have equal
status. How this actually works is still a mystery. It is only
later that these difficult issues would be addressed.

The challenge was to create a language that captured the
nature of these basic relationships that did not diminish the
power this triune God to attain a full, complete, and final
salvation of all of humanity. Now this is where it gets dicey,
because we sort of know *what is not true*, but we are (if I

---

32 Nicene Creed, US Conference of Catholic Bishops, 2012.

may slip into the vernacular here) darned if we know *what is*. Because we are talking about God here, we understand all too well that we will never plumb the depths of the reality of God from the vantage point of our temporal existence, but we still need some language that can be used to establish limits not so much on what *is* true, but what is *not* true. We need a word for the three somethings, and the word that was chosen was *person*. Unfortunately, as we reflect on Greek mythology of the gods, we know that they were thought to be separate beings who could be called *persons*, so the word points immediately toward tritheism—three gods. We will need considerable qualifying language to hem in the special meaning that we attach to this word. Before we go further to see what we mean, it is important to note the word for *that which is the same* among the three *persons* of the Trinity. The word that was chosen was *nature*. So we have three persons in one nature. Whew! That seems easy until we try to articulate what we mean by this statement. Here we are well served by the formula established by what is known as the *Quicunque Vult*[33] or the Creed of pseudo-Athanasius:

> Whosoever will be saved, before all things it is necessary that he hold the Catholic Faith.

> Which Faith except everyone do keep whole and undefiled, without doubt he shall perish everlastingly.

> And the Catholic Faith is this: That we worship one God in Trinity, and Trinity in Unity,

---

33 These are the first words of the Creed in Latin, which means "Whosoever wishes."

neither confounding the Persons, nor dividing the Substance.

For there is one Person of the Father, another of the Son, and another of the Holy Ghost.

But the Godhead of the Father, of the Son, and of the Holy Ghost, is all one, the Glory equal, the Majesty co-eternal.

Such as the Father is, such is the Son, and such is the Holy Ghost.

The Father uncreate, the Son uncreate, and the Holy Ghost uncreate.

The Father incomprehensible, the Son incomprehensible, and the Holy Ghost incomprehensible.

The Father eternal, the Son eternal, and the Holy Ghost eternal.

And yet they are not three eternals, but one eternal.

As also there are not three incomprehensibles, nor three uncreated, but one uncreated, and one incomprehensible.

So likewise the Father is Almighty, the Son Almighty, and the Holy Ghost Almighty.

And yet they are not three Almighties, but one Almighty.

So the Father is God, the Son is God, and the Holy Ghost is God.

And yet they are not three Gods, but one God.

So likewise the Father is Lord, the Son Lord, and the Holy Ghost Lord, and yet not three Lords, but one Lord.

For like as we are compelled by the Christian verity to acknowledge every Person by himself to be both God and Lord,

So are we forbidden by the Catholic Religion, to say, There be three Gods, or three Lords...

And in this Trinity none is afore, or after other; none is greater, or less than another;

But the whole three Persons are co-eternal together and co-equal.

So that in all things, as is aforesaid, the Unity in Trinity and the Trinity in Unity is to be worshipped.

He therefore that will be saved must thus think of the Trinity . . . [34]

34 *Book of Common Prayer* (New York: Seabury Press, 1979) 864–865.

Even if you don't understand the significance of all this language, is should be clear the lengths to which the Church had to go to make sure there was no watering down of the role that the Father, Son and Holy Spirit played in salvation history. Theologians are still trying to find language and analogies to make the nature of the Trinity accessible.[35]

What we are looking for is a guide to the nature of community here on earth. The question we are asking is whether the communal nature of God tells us something about our own communal nature. If community is essential to the nature of God, could it be that community is essential to our own nature? To make this connection between a triune God and our community of faith on earth, we need a good analogy for the Trinity that can shed some light on the nature of the three persons and their relationship to one another. Specifically, we are looking for *necessary* relationships—ones that must be true—to inform us about *necessary* relationships in our own lives that must be true for this argument to be compelling.

Let's start with some basics. All three persons are infinite in extent—they are not finite. They exhibit perfect unity while at the same time—and this is tricky—they are infinitely different. Why must we assert such a bizarre relationship? Even though all three persons possess fully the one divine nature, they are distinguished from each other completely in their personhood. If they were not completely different persons then we would have to argue about how different they are. We would be caught up in some discussion of levels of difference. In reality, they are completely different, even though, as we have said, this difference hinges on only two

---

35 See Walter Kasper, *The God of Jesus Christ* (New York: Continuum, 2012).

little words, *begotten* and *proceeding*. The nature of this unity in the context of diversity is an essential part of our understanding of the Trinity. The difference in the way in which this works itself out in the Godhead is that the diversity is seen to be infinite and the unity is seen to be perfectly complete. *Ha!* See if you can get your brain around that one.

This very same theme of unity in diversity is also acted out in the community of faith. As totally unique individuals gather together to express the love of Christ, and therefore become disciples of Christ, a unity grows that does not swamp the diversity but enhances it in such a way that the whole community is enhanced. Just as we are called to be "one, even as I and the Father are one" (John 17:11)—in other words, we are not only called to be in one accord in faith and activity, we are also called to live fully into the unique individuals that God created us to be with our own unique pathway into the perfect will of the Father.

We now understand that God in his very essence is *relational*, but we only need two to be in relationship. Why do we need three? One way to think about this is to see the Father begetting the Son out of love and the Son receiving that love and returning it to the Father. This giving, receiving, and returning thus becomes an essential part of the Godhead. We, therefore, have two persons of the Trinity engaged in a relationship that is based on the giving, receiving, and returning of love.[36] One way to think of this is to see the love itself as the third person of the Trinity. Why do we need to do that? First, we see the absolute necessity for two persons—a lover and a beloved—and the love that passes between

---

36 See a description of this kind of relationship in Philip Turner, *Sex, Money and Power: An Essay in Christian Social Ethics* (Cambridge: Cowley Publications, 1985), 17–20.

them. So there are clearly three "things" that must be present for God to be love *in himself*. The fact that the love takes on the status of a third person follows largely from Scripture. There does not appear to be any way to prove this status except to assert that the status was articulated by the way Jesus and the apostles talked about the Holy Spirit and the way the Holy Spirit is said to have acted in salvation history. It was clear to the early Church Fathers that Jesus intended for us to see the Holy Spirit as God and yet acting as a different entity from the Son and the Father.

From this understanding we can see that if God is love *in himself*, then creation is not an *essential* object of God's love, but creation becomes the free and unnecessary outpouring of that love. In other words, while love does not *have to create* outside itself, it is the natural consequence of love. If love were compelled to be creative, then what was created would not be a free gift. We see this very same relationship in marriage. A man and a woman, two very different people, come together in the sacrament of Holy Matrimony for the express purpose of manifesting the love of God in their relationship and thereby offering the possibility of being integral parts of the freely loving creativity of God—a creativity that has the natural potential to bring forth new life. Thus, the Trinity becomes the model for Christian marriage, and this marriage becomes, if it is done right, a model of Christian community.

Finally, we might look at how the Trinity informs our understanding of the individual. We know from Jesus' summary of the law that we are called to love our neighbors as ourselves. As we alluded to above, this means that we are called to love ourselves. *Hmmm!* Actually, when you think about it, loving ourselves becomes a bit of a conundrum. How am I as a single person supposed to love myself? What is it about the human self that makes self-love possible? Does the Father engage in self-love? If so, then why do we need a Trinity for love to be intrinsic in God? Well, this is some new territory. I will be sticking my neck out here, so bear with me and let us see where this takes us. We might begin by talking about the relation between self-love and self-consciousness. The former clearly has a positive connotation and the latter often has a somewhat negative connotation. They both, however, require the ability of the subject to reflect on him- or herself. We could say that self-love is a condition of all the parts of one's self being satisfied or at peace with all the others. This peace sounds a lot like integrity. When there is perfect integrity and all the parts are functioning as they were intended—there is a lack of internal conflict. There is a sense of peace. The bottom line would be a sense of satisfaction or even joy with who we are. While we don't go around thinking how much we love ourselves (unless you are a flaming narcissist), we certainly can spend a lot of time thinking about how we wish we were different. This dissatisfaction or lack of peace would have to be equated with a lack of self-love. Being comfortable in one's own skin is another way of describing self-love.

We might also assert that when one has a unitive experience with God, as the mystics describe, one's self-consciousness goes away. To be joyfully engaged in some activity, whether it is prayer, sports, or some creative activity like writing, building a quantitative model (that is what I do when I am not writing), cooking an exquisite soup, or rebuilding an automobile engine, is to be so absorbed that self-consciousness fades away. This kind of union may be the highest form of existential (having only to do with our existence and not with external factors) love. In other words, love seeks union with the beloved. If this is indeed so, then the highest form of self-love is existential and has nothing to do with self-reflection. The more we are self-reflecting the less we are experiencing the existential, unitive condition that is the highest form of self-love. It does, however, require an "other"—God, a manuscript, a model, a soup recipe, or an engine block. This is just as true for the love between a man and a woman. To become lost in the other is totally to lose one's self-consciousness. In intimate relationships there is clearly a sense (and again, do not ask how I know) of wanting to absorb the other into one's self—to become one. The becoming one is not the reduction of the other, but the adding to. It is very hard to describe and yet is the essence of true love—the total all-consuming desire to take the other in—to hold, honor, protect, make whole, to value every molecule of their very being. As we have said, our corporeal nature limits us in this unity. We wish to transcend the boundaries inherent in the outer limits of our bodies. This is why physical intercourse is often as close as we can come to the complete unitive experience— to physically, psychologically, and spiritually envelope the other. The height of this experience is not reached *in spite of* the differences between man and woman, but precisely *because* of the differences. It seems to be counter-intuitive to understand that through love individuality is not reduced but heightened. This does not mean that we do not need or find things in common as we grow together, but in some profound sense we simultaneously develop our own unique identities. As those identities become more and more distinctive, we approach the model of the Trinity—infinite difference in perfect union. This model of the Trinity and how this relationship between Father, Son, and Holy Spirit is manifest in the love of Christ leads us ultimately into the way we reflect this same love as his disciples within the community of faith.

13

DISCIPLESHIP

*"Go therefore and make disciples of all na-
tions, baptizing them in the name of the Father and of the Son and of the Holy Spirit."*
Matt 28:19

This is not a suggestion but a command. As Christians
this is our bounden duty—and it starts with the act of
baptism in the name of the Holy Trinity. This baptism is seen
as the essential launching pad of our journey toward Christ
and back to God. It is what makes us Christians. But what
does this journey entail. What are we supposed to look like
if we accept this challenge of being a disciple of Christ. Well,
here is the frosting on the cake, the *pièce de résistance*, the *crème
de la crème*, the *sumum bonum*. Jesus, the Second Person of the
Holy Trinity—the communion that is the deep structure and
essence of the triune God—states unequivocally:

By this all men will know that you are my

disciples, if you have love for one another. (John
13:35)

The whole reason for talking about the community of
faith is that it is the place where we learn to love as Christ
loved us and to be recognized as his disciples. As you can
see from the brief discussion above, figuring out what love
should look like in different situations is not a trivial exercise.
Many of us have a lot to learn, and many of us need a lot of
practice. The safe place for this kind of learning and practice
is the community of faith. It is also the place into which we
invite people in order to show them that same love and to
make it available to them. The degree to which we live out
this love is the degree to which we can call ourselves disciples
of Jesus Christ; the degree to which we fail to live out this
love just may be the degree to which he might say, "I never
knew you." So let us consider the possibility that our whole
Christian experience of discipleship is centered on this singular principle—to love one another as Christ has loved us. Our
worship services, prayer groups, men's and women's groups,
our book and study groups, our individual spiritual growth,
as well as our corporate service to others are all centered on
our journey to embody the love of Christ. As we develop
our understanding of the community of faith, we should at
the same time and degree be developing our understanding
of how to be disciples of Jesus Christ by our love. These two
realities are really inseparable.

We have just discussed how love can be manifest in a wide
range of ways and how the highest form of love is manifest
in the Trinity. If we desire to be recognized as Jesus' disciples
by our love, we might want to address the question of why
we would want to be his disciples in the first place. We call

disciples "followers." We know the apostles were followers and as such were a subset of all the disciples of Jesus. They were the key disciples chosen to carry forward Jesus' work, teachings, and his very being as sons of God.

Their first task was to *understand.* In order to do this, they were sent the Holy Spirit:

> When the Spirit of truth comes, he will guide you into all the truth; for he will not speak on his own authority, but whatever he hears he will speak, and he will declare to you the things that are to come. (John 16:13)

That understanding formed the entire foundation of their discipleship. While the apostles received the Holy Spirit at Pentecost, many Christian traditions believe that we receive the Holy Spirit at baptism.[37] While it would be nice if this reception involved a transfer of information, insight, wisdom, and understanding at one fell swoop, the fact is that we are given access to this understanding, but we need to work at appropriating that access. This kind of understanding is not simply intellectual, however. The apostles' first dose of understanding came from experiencing the Lord himself—his actions, his feelings, his responses to a variety of situations, and his responses to them as they encountered him and reacted to this encounter. The deeper meaning of this encounter was only accessible through faith in God. Recall Jesus'

---

37 The Catholics, Anglicans, and Orthodox view the reception of the Holy Spirit as occurring in the Sacrament of Holy Baptism and reinforced at Confirmation. Different Protestant traditions may see the reception of the Holy Spirit occurring in other ways. What we seem to agree on is the essential role that this reception plays in our respective spiritual journeys.

response to Peter, "Blessed are you, Simon Bar-Jona! For flesh and blood has not revealed this to you, but my Father who is in heaven" (Matt 16:17). A second kind of understanding would have come from the Hebrew Scriptures. Both the content and its meaning as revealed by the Holy Spirit were essential parts of the context in which they gradually accessed the meaning of what was taking place. This combination of experience, revelation, and intellectual learning in faith was the essence of their journey in and through Christ. All disciples must make this same journey.

Their second task was to be *willing* to act on the understanding they received. "If you love me you will keep my commandments" (John 14:15). This kind of obedience does not arise out of fear or constraint, but out of love, understanding, and faith. Recall that the source of their deep understanding was the Holy Spirit who was the outpouring of love from the Father and the Son. Love and truth found through understanding are therefore essentially tied together.

Finally, there was the call, not just to be *willing* to act, but to actually *do it*. "Go therefore and make disciples of all nations, baptizing them in the name of the Father and of the Son and of the Holy Spirit" (Matt 28:19). According to this directive, the beginning of a journey in Christ as a disciple is to be baptized with water in the name of the Father, Son, and Holy Spirit—the very essence of the triune God. Once this has happened and the new disciple has received the Holy Spirit, they begin the same journey as all disciples who have gone before them—a journey of understanding, love, faith, obedience, and action.

So far it looks a lot like this journey of discipleship can be done on one's own. It begins with our own personal baptism, the growth of our own personal understanding, the development of our own personal faith and willingness, and finally, our own stepping out in individual action. The central question we are addressing here is whether indeed this journey is possible alone. Could Jesus have done his work in the same way? Why did Jesus need twelve apostles? Why didn't he just go out and preach. It seemed to work for him at an early age when he preached in the Temple. It seemed to work when he preached the Sermon on the Mount. Were the apostles there for crowd control? Were they needed to handle the logistics of distributing fish and loaves? Or was it essential that someone *respond* to the Christ for anything of substance to happen at all? What if Jesus had come, and no one had listened, would we have had any Incarnation as we understand it? Would there have been any salvation history? Any redemption of mankind? While we tend to concentrate on the actions of one man, Jesus of Nazareth—the birth, life, death, resurrection, and ascension of one man—we are drawn to a staggering reality that the apostles and other disciples were an essential part of the Christ event. Not a by-line, or an interesting subplot, but absolutely unequivocally essential. The quality and character of their discipleship was foundational. They mattered. They mattered because salvation requires a savior and a "savee." It takes two to tango, and it takes at least two for the Christ event to have any meaning or efficacy—because that meaning and efficacy is all about a *relationship* between God and man—and between man and man.[38] Also, it isn't enough for two people simply to "shuffle" for there to be a legitimate tango. And it takes disciples who understand (at some level), are willing to surrender to that understanding, and to act on the basis of that

---

38 I tried to use the more general term "mankind" here, but it just didn't work.

surrender for salvation to have taken place.

We are confronted with the same kind of paradox that is reflected in the old Philosophy 101 question, "If a tree falls in the forest and there is no one around, does it make a sound?" Of course the answer depends on how one defines the word "sound." If we define it as a phenomenon of air vibrations then we could say that the answer is *yes*—the air vibrates due to the crash of the tree no matter whether there is anyone around or not. But if we define a sound as the interaction of the air vibrations with an eardrum or other sensor, then our answer would be *no*. In fact, the concept of a sound preceded the understanding of how that sound was made, and as such, it was defined in terms of the hearer. We could say the same thing about Jesus. The Christ event is defined in terms of the effect it had on those who encountered him. We call this salvation history. Only later did the Gospel writers and theologians try to understand the dynamics of that event—what it *was* in itself and not so much in terms of what it *did*. People were saved first, and only later did they try to understand how or why they were saved. It was clear that this process of salvation required a savior and one who is being saved. Thus, salvation can and must be defined in terms of a *relationship*. If there were no one to hear the words of salvation and respond to them, there would have been no salvation—zippo. In other words, the disciples were not just there for some ancillary function related to the Christ event—they were an essential part of the event. Not only must we assert that the disciples mattered, but we are compelled to say that they were fundamental.

One of the most difficult things for us to understand in our own personal journey is that we also matter—that our lives are not just about ourselves, but intimately affect and are affected by all those around us. If we are convinced that the disciples of Jesus mattered in salvation history, we are then led to the question whether our own discipleship matters in the continuing salvation history that is being played out here and now. Do we live our lives as if we matter? Unfortunately, we often look at the world as something to be sampled as we see fit. We go to the movies we want to see, and no one seems to be the wiser. No one jumps up in the movie theater and says to me, "Jonathan, I am so very glad you came. You have made my movie experience immeasurably better by your presence." I just sit there in the dark, watch the movie, and quietly leave the theater with all the other theatergoers, walk to my car, and drive home. No big whoop. The same may be true at church. I park my car, enter the church, participate in the service, maybe if I am lucky I say hello to a friend or acquaintance or even the pastor, go back to my car, and go home. If there is Sunday school I may attend if the topic suits me, but I have no sense that I will be missed. I do not mean that my absence will simply be *noted*, but that those present will be the poorer for my absence. I really am not convinced that *I matter.*

Sometimes we look at the whole modern Christian drama being played out throughout the world as something we can dip our ladles into and taste as we are moved to do so. Atheists think they can do without tasting at all. Some who call themselves Christians use a teaspoon on holidays, and some use a tablespoon on Sundays, while others fill up their jugs and quaff down copious amounts of spiritual "drink" every day of their lives. But few of us view our imbibing as necessary to the very process of which we are partaking—that we somehow have something to do with the very drink itself. We believe that the process of Christianity and its associated salvation of humanity will go on with or without us. We can take it or leave it—and no one will be the richer or poorer.

What we are suggesting is that this is simply not true. The idea that this kind of individualistic interpretation will yield *life at its deepest level* has never been true. It wasn't true from the very beginning through the early stages of Judaism, it wasn't true during the three years of Jesus' ministry on earth, and it isn't true today. We all matter, even if neither we, nor those around us, believe it. One way to think of this is to consider a fabric made up of thousands of threads that are the weft and warp of the material—the crossing threads that are the very nature of the fabric.[39] We all have seen what happens to our jeans when a single thread is broken. The hole gradually grows and grows, often to our delight, until only one set of threads is keeping the jeans from totally disintegrating. A bed sheet that suffers the smallest of nicks will soon have to be discarded or patched. In other words, each thread is essential to the integrity of the whole, and without that integrity the whole is mortally wounded.

If the community of faith is the fabric of our lives in Christ, when that fabric is damaged even slightly, not only don't we see the damage, but we don't even know where to look to find the thread that has been injured. The wound can continue to grow unabated and unnoticed until the whole is no more. This may be because there *is* no recognizable whole. We cannot see how the weft and warp of all the individual members lock together to create an integrated whole because we have failed to weave the fabric. It could be that all we have is a pile of loose, worn, and broken threads that

39 Technically the warp is made up of the stationary threads on a loom, and the weft is made up of the threads that are at right angle to the warp that are introduced by the back and forth movement of the shuttle.

cannot function as they were initially intended. If we press this analogy, we can see that we need to develop three capacities: the first is the capacity to weave together the threads of the community of faith, the second is the capacity to recognize a wound in the fabric of our Christian community, and the third is the capacity to know how to mend it. To do this we must first believe that there *is* a fabric of which we are a part, whether we know it or like it or not. This is the community of faith whose threads are woven together by Christian discipleship—the sharing of experience, faith, understanding, will, and action. Furthermore, the premise being posited here is that the community of faith is the place to recognize those wounds and the place where they are mended. If we are to be worthy of the name "disciples of Christ" we must know that we matter, understand when our wounds impact the life of the community of faith, and how the Christian community of faith can be a source—maybe the only source—of true healing—not only of ourselves, but also of the fabric of the community itself.

14

THE COMMUNITY OF FAITH

Our faith tells us, at least implicitly, that the whole mystery of life is based on truth and love, and that the greatest expression of that truth and love was a man who lived two thousand years ago—Jesus of Nazareth. Who he was in his earthly ministry is the quintessential model for not only our lives as individuals or even our life in a much broader sense as the Body of Christ—the Church universal—but also particularly the model for the community of faith. How did he and the apostles operate? How did they teach and learn, pray and play, experience conflict and peace, practice and grow, and ultimately become transformed into the people whom the Father wanted them to be? Notice that I included Jesus in this process of community building. While the Christology of Jesus Christ as both teacher and participant may be beyond the scope of this little work, we should at least assert that if he is to be the perfect model for our human existence in its highest form, he must model both roles as leader and participant. We might be hard pressed to squeeze out the participant part if we place him high on a pedestal, but we should at least pay attention to those moments in Scripture in which he shows this aspect of his ministry.

> Then he poured water into a basin, and began to wash the disciples' feet, and to wipe them with the towel with which he was girded. (John 13:5)

> No longer do I call you servants, for the servant does not know what his master is doing; but I have called you friends, for all that I have heard from my Father I have made known to you. (John 15:15)

> And stretching out his hand toward his disciples, he said, "Here are my mother and my brothers! For whoever does the will of my Father in heaven is my brother, and sister, and mother." (Matt 12:49–50)

> For those whom he foreknew he also predestined to be conformed to the image of his Son, in order that he might be the first-born among many brethren. (Rom 8:29)

He evidently wanted us to see him not only as Lord and Master, but also as servant and friend—even brother. The challenge associated with playing the dual role of leader and participant is a bit of a mystery, but we should be used to mysteries by now. How God can become man is really the same kind of question as how Lord can become brother. This theme of being both leader and participant will form for us an essential aspect of our model of the community of faith. For us to try to walk the walk of both leader and participant is in some remote sense to be penetrating ever so slightly this mystery. Once we appreciate to some extent how Jesus understood the way he related to his followers, we can go on to see how Paul and the other apostles operated in building and functioning in the early Christian communities.

It appears that the earliest Christian gentile communities met in people's houses. Although we don't have a record of the exact numbers, from the tone of Paul's letters, we might assume that they were larger than the "small faith groups" of today. We also know that these communities grew rather rapidly. From the Acts of the Apostles, we know that they shared material goods and worshiped together, so we can also assume a high level of intimacy. We also know that Paul wrote to these communities to encourage, teach, and admonish them in the faith and that these letters were passed around and studied among the various communities. Although the kind of persecution experienced by these groups varied from time and place, the execution of both Paul and Peter would indicate that there was always some pressure on these groups to maintain a low profile. This pressure would also result in a heightened level of identification within the community. We will see that these characteristics of sharing, learning, worship, and intimacy are all essential aspects of the kind of community of faith we are describing here—the experience of which is focused on leading lives at their deepest and most rewarding levels.

In today's complex world, as we live our lives in the context of joy, suffering, pain, compassion, warmth, pride, envy, anger, gentleness, and so forth—if and only if we are paying attention—we will learn something about what this life is all about. Like a mixture of oil and water in which the oil will eventually rise to the surface, in a life of such a mixture of goodness and not-so-goodness, truth and love will always find their way to the surface—maybe slowly in gentle puffs, maybe in feeble spurts, maybe in lurches and quakes, or maybe in torrents that overwhelm us, but inevitably—if we let it—erupting in glory, delight, and wonder.

The community of faith, therefore, foreshadows an idealized world where things work as they were intended and people care about each other. The community of faith is supposed to function "on earth as it is in heaven." We pray for this all the time in the Lord's Prayer (the "Our Father" for Catholics), but we never seem to pull it off. In other words, I have never actually seen a real community of faith as I believe Jesus intended it to be in all its fullness and glory. I have seen glimmers and pieces and pointers to the incredible possibilities, but I have never seen all the pieces functioning together. I will assume that, even in the midst of misunderstanding, posturing, and betrayal, Jesus intended that he and the Twelve Apostles function as an authentic, albeit embryonic, community of faith, and I will postulate that the early church communities—the communities in Rome, Corinth, Galatia, Ephesus, Philippi, Colossae, Thessalonica, and those in Jerusalem functioned as budding communities of faith, especially with the help of Paul and Peter poking at them, admonishing them, teaching them, and living with them. It is only from our current vantage point, however, that we can begin to see all the pieces of an authentic community of faith and how they might fit together. It is only by trying to fit these pieces together in a rapidly changing socio-economic environment that we begin to appreciate the depth of the Christian calling and the daunting hurdles that must be overcome.

The Christian community of faith is very different from what we usually think of as a congregation or even a small faith group. Neither is it a "program" in the normal sense of the word. A comment by Father Hayes Rockwell, former rector of St. James Episcopal Church in Manhattan, seems to capture one aspect of the dilemma: "Holy Communion is a *reflection* of community, it does not *create* community." For example, we Christians can go to church, even take communion until we are blue in the face, and never know the names of the folks sitting beside us, let alone engage them in any meaningful way. While Holy Communion certainly nourishes, strengthens, and deepens our common life as it represents a shared meaning and a common love of God, it cannot create that communal life by itself. Some may spend hours in the adoration chapel[40] and go on many silent retreats and still not be a member of a Christian community of faith. We can be a member of the choir, the altar guild, the Ignatian spirituality group, the youth group, the church-sponsored Boy or Girl Scout troop, the soup kitchen, the welcoming committee, the men's organization, the women's organization, the Bible study group, the Christian Education Committee, the environmental protection group, the gay rights group,

---

40 For Catholic and Orthodox Christians, the host or sacramental bread of the Eucharist, once it has been consecrated, becomes the body, blood, soul, and divinity of Jesus Christ. This transformation is called *transubstantiation*. As such it is worthy of adoration or worship. The adoration chapel is a place where Catholics can go to pray or meditate in the presence of Jesus himself in the form of the consecrated Host. Protestants tend not to go that far in their understanding of the Host. Anglicans, Lutherans, and Methodists would be comfortable talking about the *real presence* of Christ in the Eucharist. Other Protestants might view the bread of the Lord's Supper as symbolic of Christ's passion. However it is viewed, the bread of the Lord's Supper is special and draws Christians of all kinds to a recollection of the precious gift that was offered us through the passion of Jesus Christ.

the anti-gay rights group, the Christians for gun control, the Christians against gun control, the right to life group, or the right to choose group and still not be a member of a true Christian community of faith. We can be a Sunday school teacher, a Eucharistic minister, a lay reader, or even a pastor and still not be a member of a true Christian community of faith. You might even be a member of a congregation with considerable fellowship and miss the deep transformative nature of a true community of faith. You might, in fact, be on the right track and not yet know exactly where the track is leading or how to proceed along it. Clearly, some are much further along this track than others, but I hope we can press enough to open all of our eyes to greater possibilities.

If the community of faith is not a program or group with a specific worthwhile purpose or mission, then what is it? If it is not just one more ministry, one more covered-dish supper, one more bazaar or one more parish picnic, then what is it? We often use the words *fellowship* and *community* interchangeably, but when we add the *of faith* qualifier, we are tightening up our picture of what we are talking about considerably. If we are asserting that it is essential to our lives as Christians and yet it is not what we usually spend our time doing as a member of a Christian congregation, then we had better have a clear understanding not only of how these other programs are *not* such a community, but why. More specifically we need to know what a true Christian community of faith looks like. What are its characteristics and how should we recognize folks who are a member of such a community.

In fact, Jesus left no ambiguity concerning this last question. We are to be recognized as his disciples by our love for one another. Well, that seems simple enough. We have talked about what that love looks like, so as long as we know that and practice it, all our various church services and ministries must be working. The central problem is that we really *don't* know the deepest manifestations of that love—the posture of joy, transparency, courage, and total submission to the truth. Few of us get there, and the reason we don't get there is the same reason that our high school soccer team never won the state championship or our college basketball team never made it to the Sweet Sixteen or why I never played first chair trombone in the New York Philharmonic. We either didn't have the talent, or the desire, or we didn't practice enough. The beauty of Christianity is that we all have the talent. Isn't that an interesting concept? We all start out our Christian journey once we are baptized as if we were child prodigies with all the talent we need to reach the highest pinnacle of "success." This is true because Christian "success" is not *measured* in the same way worldly success is measured. In addition, Christian "success" is not *achieved* in the same way worldly success is achieved. Christian success is directly tied to our likeness to a certain individual—not a person with particular skills, but a person who had a particular relationship both to us and to the Father. Ultimately, our Christian journey is about growing in our likeness to Jesus Christ, and the achievement of that goal is dependent only on our ability to allow Jesus Christ to direct the traffic.

But there is one very strong similarity with a worldly quest for success, namely, we grow in our relationship with Jesus Christ through a concrete set of processes—we call them spiritual exercises—which look much like sitting at the piano and practicing Chopin's *Prelude in E Minor*. To get better, we practice, practice, practice. Not only do we practice, however, but we must also learn what to practice. We have teachers and coaches to guide us. We must learn

the correct finger positions on the piano, the correct bow-
ings on the violin, the correct way to throw the football, the
correct way of breathing for singing, the correct way to use
our hands for massage. If the same thing is true for those of
us committed to our journey in Christ, what does this deliberate approach to learning and practice look like? All these
other worldly endeavors are easily evaluated. Either you can
play Rachmaninov's *Prelude in C# Minor*—or you can't. Either you can throw a tight spiral forward pass 40 yards and
hit the receiver—or you can't. Either you can dance the lead
role in *Swan Lake*—or you can't. Either you can sing *Nessun
Dorma*—or you can't. Certainly there are qualities of each of
these—brilliance, accuracy, sonority, and feeling, but they
come after learning basic execution. Next we are challenged
to play like Arthur Rubinstein, pass like John Elway, dance
like Ana Pavlova, or sing like Luciano Pavarotti. In the case
of our Christian walk, our challenge is a bit different. All we
as Christians have to do is to live our lives like Jesus Christ—
and we believe that by doing that we are accessing the best
that life has to offer. Conceptually this looks like it might be
easy. We have the "talent"—now all we need to do is figure
out what and how to *practice*. Herein lies the rub. We are
talking about the art of life, and this art is more accessible
and yet much more subtle than the skills of a great pianist,
singer, dancer, or quarterback. The community of faith is all
about forming us into the equivalent of Rubensteins, Elways,
Pavlovas, and Pavarottis in the practice of *life*.

   While we may take life for granted, it should be just as
clear that some do better at life than others. Serial killers
flunk life. Mass murderers flunk life. Bernie Madoff and others who spend their time trying to cheat others flunk too.
People who spend their whole lives criticizing and blaming

others probably get lower grades. People who are completely self-centered get low marks—and so forth. So our challenge in the community of faith is to get high marks on the practice of life, recognizing that the one who got the highest "score" was Jesus himself—the way, the truth, and the life. He showed us what life is all about—and that happens to be love. It is not just any love, however, but his own love.

Once we understand that practicing is our goal, the challenge is to figure out what the "finger positions" of life are and then how to practice them. What are the basic functions of a community of faith that we can practice? While undoubtedly the following list is not exhaustive, it is at least a start at getting at the challenge before us. As we penetrate the meaning behind the items on this list, we might then be able to clarify for ourselves why ministries and programs are not communities of faith and how to start to build something that truly is. As we expand on these functions, we should appreciate better the potential as well as the challenges of creating an authentic community of faith.

> 1. To have a true and vital **experience**—to know our fellow Christians as travelers on the same journey toward fullness in Christ.

> 2. To **share** our journey with our fellow pilgrims, so that each may be lifted up and edified.

> 3. To **learn** the profound truths found in the Christian deposit of faith that guide us into the way, the truth, and the life associated with our lives in Christ.

4. To engage in open and charitable **dialogue** that seeks only the truth of God and the consequent enlightenment of each member of the community.

5. To **practice** living out our relationships toward others as we deepen our transformation into the likeness of Jesus Christ.

6. To **pray** together as an expression of our vital relationship to Father, Son, Holy Spirit, and to each other.

7. To learn to **play**—to engage each other with a light-hearted spirit of joy and delight that reflects a serious search for the truth without taking ourselves too seriously.

8. To learn **accountability**—to learn to understand that each of us is important to the life of the others and that the actions of one influence the lives of all the others.

9. To learn the pathway of **discernment** by learning to be open to the promptings of the Holy Spirit.

10. To **minister** to others in times of need.

11. To **evangelize** both within and outside our own congregation so that others might participate in the rich and joy-filled experience of what

it means to be a member of a Christian community of faith.

12. To search for opportunities and connections
for meaningful **ecumenism**—the process of
uniting the various expressions of the Christian
faith in Jesus Christ.

If we think of these functions as a kind of lens through
which we can view all of our church activities, we should
be able to see how programs and ministries are usually too
focused, albeit on important goals, to be considered as substitutes for an authentic community of faith. It should be clear
that the choir, while offering some of these aspects of community, is mainly focused on singing. While the Ignatian
spirituality group may have a few other aspects of community, its emphasis is on a life of prayer and service. While the
soup kitchen may stress ministry to others, it probably does
not engage in purposeful dialogue. Each program, if viewed
through this lens may be seen to fall short of the true full-
blown, high-octane community of faith. This observation
does not in any way invalidate these activities—they are essential parts of the expression of our Christian life. What we
must *not* do, however, is to confuse ourselves by believing
that we have something that we do not have. These twelve
functions just indicate that we may need more than simply a
plethora of programs and ministries, if we are to develop into
disciples whom Jesus would recognize.

PART III

THE FIT, FEEL, AND FINISH OF THE COMMUNITY OF FAITH

15

A METAPHOR

As we discussed earlier, there are a number of functions that begin to operate as a true Christian community of faith starts to form. Notice that I said "starts," because a fully-formed community is really what Jesus was talking about when he referred to the Kingdom of God on earth—a new order defined not only by the way we relate to one another, but also by the way God's reign is being fully realized—a cosmic as well as an earthly order. When we pray in the Lord's Prayer, "as it is in heaven," we are not only praying for a total conversion as individuals, but also a total conversion of how we relate to God and to one another—where God's Love and God's Truth reign supreme. The locus of this change in the earthly order and how it relates to the cosmic order is the Christian community of faith. It is in this community of faith that we start to get the look and feel of the Kingdom of God on earth. It is here that we take baby steps, eat mushed-up baby food, and start to grow into the people who we are intended to be. It is here that the eternal meets the temporal, and the mystery of God meets the mystery of

man in Christ. We can get a hint of the nature of our own
progressive journey and ultimate goal from Paul:

> I fed you with **milk**, not solid food; for you
> were not ready for it; and even yet you are not
> ready . . . (1 Cor 3:2)

> I have fought the good fight, I have finished the
> race, I have kept the faith. (2 Tim 4:7)

In other words, we should be striving to move beyond
baby food and uncoordinated flabby muscles to strong, more
robust nourishment, one that can build muscles with which
we can fight the fight and run the race. To be able to keep
the faith, we need the spiritual equivalent of a strong, healthy
body. To build this kind of spiritual health is not an easy process—it takes time and deliberate effort. More importantly,
we cannot do it alone. I do not merely mean that it is hard-
er or not as much fun alone. I mean it is absolutely *impossible* to do it alone—because the process of being transformed
into the perfect likeness of Jesus Christ is centered on the
Eleventh Commandment. This transformation is centered
on love, and just like the tango, it takes at least two. As you
will see, the process actually takes quite a bit more than two,
because it involves a deliberate struggle with those toward
whom we may not feel a great deal of sympathy or compat-
ibility. Finally, Bible studies and other Sunday school classes
per se are not substitutes. Choral and other ministries *per se*
are not substitutes. And yet communities of faith can grow
out of them, but with considerable effort. The very nature of
the community of faith precludes a purpose other than itself.
It is its own reason for being. While learning and ministry

are part of the package, they are not its central *raison d'etre*—
its very reason for being. The community of faith is its own
reason for being, with its goal being our personal transformation into the perfect likeness of Jesus Christ and our communal goal being the manifestation of the Kingdom of God on
earth. But this goal is not external to the community, but its
very essence. In other words, the community, in some deeply
spiritual sense, *is* the goal. If that is true, then we need to do
much more work to understand the nature of this kind of
community.

In the automobile business, the concept of the *fit, feel,
and finish* refers to the way the parts fit together, the way
the car feels as a result of the proper fit of the parts, and the
overall appearance that results from both the fit and feel.
Here we will be squeezing these concepts as a metaphor
for the different dimensions of a fully-functional Christian
community of faith. First we will discuss some of the key
functions of a community of faith that must be developed
over time. We are calling it the "fit" of the community of
faith—the basic parts and how they fit together. It is only
when we see these parts begin to work together that we
can start to sense we are on the right track—that we are
moving toward the "feel" of the community of faith. The
"feel" has to do with the way in which the community of
faith changes our perspective, adjusts our sensibilities, and
enhances our ability to love the way Christ loved. This feel
should ultimately embody the peace of God that passes all
understanding—which itself moves us toward the final "finish" in Christ. Our "finish" as a Christian community of
faith comes from the degree to which we look, feel, and act
like Jesus Christ—the way in which we live into the perfect likeness of Jesus Christ—*together*. That finish is bright,

gentle to the touch, without "spot or blemish."

> Therefore, beloved, since you wait for these, be zealous to be found by him without spot or blemish, and at peace. (2 Pet 3:14)

In other words, it is the light of Christ that shines forth. It is the glory of God that spreads outward and proclaims to the world that Jesus Christ is Lord. I hope all this will be clearer as we move through the *fit, feel,* and *finish* of an authentic Christian community of faith.

16

THE "FIT" OF CHRISTIAN COMMUNITY

The fit of a community of faith involves those functions that can be seen, guided, and to some degree, evaluated. They involve experience, sharing, learning, dialogue, practice, praying, playing, accountability, discernment, ministry, evangelization, and ecumenism. In other words, we can manage them. We can make sure that there are opportunities for each of these to take place. We cannot necessarily manage the way these influence the deeper rivers of spirituality that move within the community and the individuals that make it up, but they can make the flow possible. While they do not offer a blueprint for community, they do provide us with the scaffolding from which a true community can be built. By these functions we are simply planting and watering with the hope that God will give the increase.

EXPERIENCE TOGETHER

The history of the faith is replete with examples of those who had a profound experience of God. In the Hebrew Bible, we could mention Moses on Mt. Sinai, or Samuel's call by the Lord, or Jacob wrestling with God, or Abraham arguing with God over the destruction of Sodom. In the New Testament, we certainly must mention the Transfiguration and Paul's encounter with the risen Lord on the road to Damascus. In modern times, we could talk about the experiences of the Virgin Mary by Saint Bernadette and Saint Catherine Labouré and the unitive experiences of God by Saint Teresa of Avila and Saint John of the Cross. All of these individual experiences declare a vital relationship between man and God. *Relationship, relationship, relationship!* The pinnacle of the Christian understanding of the centrality of relationship is the Holy Trinity, through which the three persons—Father, Son, and Holy Spirit—reflect God as essentially being a loving *relationship* in himself.

But what about experiences of God within the Christian community? Well, the first would be the experience of the apostles as they lived in relationship with and grew in their understanding of Jesus Christ. This experience is culminated by the words of Peter when asked by Jesus, "Who do you say that I am?" To which Peter responds, "You are the Messiah, the son of the living God." Jesus then gives us a stunning conclusion regarding that experience: "Blessed are you, Simon son of Jonah, for flesh and blood has not revealed this to you, but my Father in heaven" (Matt 16:13–17). Thus, the experience of Jesus resulted in a deep encounter with God on a number of different levels. Since this encounter is what we would call the first Christian community of faith, we take the relationship between Jesus and his immediate followers as our model for all subsequent communities including those at Jerusalem, Corinth, Ephesus, Philippi, Thessalonica, Galatia,

Colossae, and Rome—as well as Denver, Clarkesville, Columbia, New York, State College, Grand Junction, Aiken,
and all other places where people gather in Christ's name.
Notice, as we stated above, that Paul's letters were to communities of faith. It was in community that individuals found
their identity as followers of Jesus Christ.

So what has happened to us today? Somehow we have
lost that deep dependence on community that was natural
in more primitive societies, including those of the Church
up to the Industrial Revolution. Early agrarian America still
had a strong identification with its small interdependent farm
communities. When the factory system of production started to pull people off the farm and out of those tightly knit
communities, dependence on each other transformed into
dependence on the industrial employer. As industrialization
progressed—and this did not occur overnight—these ancient
bonds gradually atrophied. Industrial towns in Pennsylvania and Ohio still had strong Christian communities with
a church practically "on every corner," but as the supply of
clergy declined, secularization progressed, and the vast array
of alternative "communities" (e.g. recreational clubs and special interest groups) evolved, many Christian churches had to
consolidate to survive. The communal structure of the parish
was gradually changed from the center of community life to
only one among many aspects of a Christian's life. Christians
at least perceived that they could find community in many
places other than the local church. What they and the larger
Church may have failed to realize was that this dilution of
attention had resulted in a total loss of the original vision
of one's "life in Christ" as the central organizing principle
of *all life*. Without the community of faith and its attendant
goals, individuals lost sight of the point of their Christian

journey—their experience of Christ *within* the community of faith.

We need only look at a modern example to understand how we might go about reclaiming that experience. The lyrics from the television show *Cheers* gives us a simple vision:

> *Sometimes you want to go*
> *where everybody knows your name,*
> *and they're always glad you came.*
> *You wanna be where you can see,*
> *our troubles are all the same*
> *You wanna be where everybody knows*
> *your name.*[41]

This universal yearning for community can be anesthetized by television (with the possible exception of great shows like *Cheers*), sporting events, and recreation to the point that we no longer think that being in a place where "everybody knows your name" is desirable or necessary, let alone even possible. Jesus, however, would no doubt declare unequivocally that the Body of Christ is just such a place. The Church of Jesus Christ, if understood in terms of adopted children of God acting out their Christ-calling, is nothing if not a place where everyone is glad to see you, where we all recognize our common journey and troubles, and at least have the desire to know each other's names and a willingness to try to learn them. Some have called the Christian community of faith a place of "hard-core caring"[42]—a place where everyone

---

41 Gary Portnoy, *Cheers*, NBC (1982–1993), Charles/Burrows/Charles Productions and Paramount Network Television.

42 Actually this came from my sister, Penny—my precious fellow traveler in the Christian faith.

is committed not only to their own personal transformation into the perfect likeness of Jesus Christ, but also to help others who are on the same journey.

While we can interpret many of these thoughts in terms of our own personal journey, the central point here is that the community of faith is indeed experiential. If we don't experience the love of Christ, then whether it is there under some kind of bushel basket is irrelevant. Love is to be experienced. Folks stay in a community of faith not for intellectual reasons, but for experiential reasons. Somehow they have experienced the love of Christ in each other. Folks may be drawn into community because of stimulating conversation or delightful jocularity—but they often do not stay for those reasons only. They stay because the love of Christ *itself* shines through all these other functions. If others do not experience the love of Christ in our community of faith, we have flunked *Community 101* and therefore we have flunked *Love 101.* And if we have flunked love, then we have flunked *Christianity 101* and have betrayed the gift of life offered to us through the Incarnation—the life, death, resurrection, and ascension of Jesus Christ. He might just say that he never knew us. On that cheerful note, let's look at some other functions of a community of faith that Jesus might recognize.

SHARE TOGETHER

One of the most striking characteristics of the early Church communities was that everything was held in common. In other words, they shared everything: their wealth, their furnishings, their food, *and* their lives. This kind of radical lifestyle even in the days of Jesus was not common. We might speculate that Jesus' parents, Joseph and Mary, were not part of such a community. While the Jewish communities of that time were close knit, all indications are that they were structured more like our communities today—made up of independent families that took responsibility for their own livelihoods, income, living spaces, and food. Joseph was a carpenter and earned income from his vocation. Tradition asserts that Jesus learned the trade from his father and was himself a carpenter by trade.

We might presume that the roots of the communal life-style of the early Christian communities can be traced to the fundamental teachings of Jesus that emphasized a willingness to offer your coat to strangers in need, to give to the poor, and to protect the widows and orphans. The story of the Good Samaritan is just one of many pointers toward a radi-cally loving and generous lifestyle that was to characterize the early Church. In fact, one of the features of these com-munities that attracted new converts was their charity—not merely charity as love, but charity demonstrated in the ac-tion of giving. This radical willingness to give was simply a consequence of the radical transformation Jesus called his followers into—a transformation into a complete surrender to the will of the Father that Jesus modeled all the way to the cross. The logical extension of such a transformation of will was a loss of attachment to the material things of this world, and this loss of attachment resulted in a willingness to share whatever you had with anyone in need.

Today, we have gotten away from this kind of radi-cal communal living among average every-day Christians. There are examples of intentional communal lifestyles de-signed to reflect this kind of radical transformation, but they are rare. One example with which I am familiar was a com-munity formed by Episcopal Bishop William Frey in Denver in the mid-1980s. I do not know the details except that the actress Ann B. Davis, who played the housekeeper Alice in the television series *The Brady Bunch,* was a member of that community. In general, however, we still see our lifestyle as autonomous in our private lives and to varying degrees communal in our church lives. This dichotomy almost inherently provides the basis for conflict between this desire for autonomy and the objectives centered on building the community of faith.

On the other hand, we do see many intentional religious communities within the Catholic, Anglican, and Orthodox traditions. Benedictine, Dominican, and Franciscan nuns, brothers, and priests represent but a small fraction of the many religious orders that reflect a wide range of communal lifestyles. Some are completely cloistered and contemplative, such as the Discalced Carmelites; others are cloistered but have clear communal vocations, as in the case of the Cistercians (Trappists); while yet others find their vocations largely "in the world," such as the Society of Jesus (Jesuits), through missionary or teaching vocations. Each order has one or more "charisms" that characterize the way in which they follow Christ, but in each case community—an intimate sharing of goods, living facilities, spiritual life and vocations—is of fundamental importance.

While most of us are, in general, not engaged in segregated communal living or in a radical sharing of goods and activities, we do understand that sharing at some level is foundational to our Christian walk. We share our time and skills through various ministries and we share our wealth through donations to our respective churches and charities of our choice. As a result of much modern psychological self-help literature, we also see sharing in terms of sharing ourselves with others. The idea of a faith-sharing group arises from this recognition that sharing ourselves is an important aspect of our faith journey.

The questions we are raising here relate to the importance of this sharing of self in the community of faith, the impediments to that sharing, and the ways in which we can enhance this aspect of our community life. Why is sharing of "self" important? One way to think of this question is to recall the statement from Paul, "For now we see in a mirror dimly, but then face to face. Now I know in part; then I shall understand fully, even as I have been fully understood" (1 Cor 13:12). This problem of seeing dimly is one of the most fundamental aspects of our earthly lives. This challenge of "seeing" clearly is most pronounced when we try to see or discern the will of God. Sometimes we cannot tell whether God is saying, "Get the rake!" or "Bake the cake!" How do we know that we are "seeing" or hearing the truth? Because each of us brings something unique to the table—a different set of skills, a different perspective, and a different ability to integrate ideas—we need each other. The only way we can help each other is to *share*— share our thoughts, our feelings, our experiences, our failures, our anxieties, our successes, our joys—the whole ball of wax. It is only through transparency of self that we can inform and edify each other's lives and help each other to *see more clearly.*

Why is this often so hard? Many of us are inherently introverts. We reluctantly reveal what we think, how we feel, and ultimately who we are to others. There may be many reasons for this. In our families, as we were growing up, we may have found a brutal reception to this kind of honesty. If those around us were insecure in their own being, the chances are good that they would have taken a certain perverse consolation in our own discomfort. The advertisement for Dove soap in which we hear, "My name is John Elway, and I am comfortable in my own skin," implies that many of us are *not* comfortable in our own skins. But where do we get this kind of comfort? All too often it comes from those around us. If they are comfortable with us, then we are comfortable with ourselves. Parents, friends, and possibly even members of our communities of faith offer us real tangible aid in feeling the comfort that ultimately leads to transparency of self—the ability and willingness to share who we are with others so that they, too, might share who they are with us.

Thus, the reluctance to share ourselves can be overcome by being in connection with those who are willing to share *themselves*. This process of gradual transformation takes time, commitment, and trust. These three factors are related. Few of us reach a state of trust immediately. It is only over a period of time that we learn who we can trust and who we cannot. But trust does not come only through time; it comes through consistency. If I always see the same person waiting for the same subway train each day, and we start a conversation that turns into a friendship, we can assert unequivocally that the relationship is based on trust that itself is based on consistency—a kind of commitment to that time and space, a connection that starts to yield personal transparency.

One of the most profound philosophical concepts in this regard came from that deeply introspective television show *Dobie Gillis*.[43] In the show, Zelda Gilroy proclaims—to Dobie's dismay—that he will eventually fall in love with her as a result of "propinquity"—the *nearness* that she continually orchestrates. She was no dummy. The consistency of that nearness always

---

43 I'm just kidding. For those of you who have not seen it, the show, on CBS from 1959–1963, was a frolicking comedy based on the many loves and other dilemmas of a teenager struggling to extricate himself from his perpetual state of confusion as he bumbled his way through life.

offers the possibility that two people will learn to trust one another, will become more and more transparent, and ultimately
will develop at least some form of affection as a result of a
deeper understanding of the other's struggles in life—struggles
that are common to all of us.

Consequently, we must note the importance of consistency
in the evolution of a true community of faith. If we are to
develop the trust necessary to yield transparency, we must be
consistent in our participation. To say, "I will show up, if I
can," means that I not only do not understand the great gift of
the love of Christ, but also am unwilling to do what it takes to
access that gift. Building the high level of trust that is compat-
ible with a sharing, open Christian community takes time and
commitment.

LEARN TOGETHER

Because we do not inherently understand the value of experience and sharing, as well as all the other aspects of the love of
Christ, we have a lot to *learn*. First, we must learn who the
incarnate Lord was,[44] if he is to be our model. This is no mean
task, because there are a number of misconceptions that either
separate him from us by overstressing his divinity or make him
ineffectual as a savior by making him so much like us that he
can't take us anywhere. Learning the balance that the Church
has struck over the last two thousand years is a daunting challenge. To do this we need to read and discuss Scripture and

---

44 Note that we must be very careful when we use the words "was" and
"is" regarding Jesus. Jesus "was" incarnate over two thousand years ago,
but upon his ascension, his humanity was drawn into the life of God for
all eternity, both past and present. For us in this life, it is the Christ who
"is" who makes possible our transformation into the incarnate Lord who
"was" when he was present on earth. This is the eternal mystery of the
Incarnation.

documents related to our faith, not simply to learn in order to *accept,* but also to learn in order to *think critically*—discerning falsehood from truth.

I grew up with the fundamental legal adage, "Ignorance of the law is no excuse." The same thing is true for our faith. Imagine that I am standing before God on the Day of Judgment and am questioned concerning the shabby way I operated on so many occasions. My response might be that I did not know any better. I can distinctly hear the pound of the gavel and the words, "Guilty as charged!" Laziness and lack of interest are no excuse for a shabby way of life based on ignorance. We all have an obligation to learn.

In the early Gentile Christian communities, members learned through the preaching and especially through the letters of Paul. They did not collect the letters in a nice box with a sentimental pink ribbon on it, but they read them over and over in order to discern their full meaning and to live out that meaning. If learning had not been such an essential part of the early communities of faith, we would not even have those letters, as well as the Gospels, the letters of Peter, James, John, and the letter to the Hebrews. We have been given a precious gift for our edification—and we ignore that gift at our own peril.

But learning takes on many forms. Learning Scripture is a good thing. Learning from other documents related to our faith is also important, but there are things to be learned simply by being a part of an evolving community of faith. Scott Peck wrote an important treatment of the development of community, entitled *The Different Drum: Community Making and Peace.*[45] According to Peck, we run a great risk if we barge

45 M. Scott Peck, *The Different Drum: Community Making and Peace* (New York: Simon and Schuster, 1987).

into a process like that of community building without being
prepared for the inevitable challenges. Building a community
of faith is not a program like Meals on Wheels or a ministry like the choir. It is not a lecture course or even a Bible
study. All of these can be orchestrated with firm leadership and
a well-defined set of content and objectives. The building of
community has one kicker that the others might not necessarily have—the activity of the Holy Spirit. No Spirit—no community. This means that the growth of the community is a bit
messy and the potential potholes are many. Peck notes:

> There can be no vulnerability without risk; there
> can be no community without vulnerability; there
> can be no peace—and ultimately no life—without
> community.[46]

Peck describes a process of evolution that involves the
movement from crisis to crisis. At each stage either the community flies apart or it grows to a new depth of transparency
and trust. Each crisis arises out of a lack of satisfaction with
the existing level of openness and honesty. A member takes
a risk by pointing out the limitations of the community and
effectively demands that the community come to terms with
the crisis of identity that has been placed on the table. If the
community rises to the challenge, the community grows. The
only alternative is for the community to disband or for the
community to "expel"[47] the troublesome member.[48] Now, not

46 Ibid., 233.
47 Some might use the term "excommunicate" in a Christian community,
but this term only means that one is no longer "in communion" with the
community and is therefore restricted from participating in "communion."
Therefore, excommunication is not synonymous with expulsion.
48 Peck, *The Different Drum*, 86–106.

all troublesome members facilitate growth, so sometimes expulsion is necessary for the community to continue to exist. It is this open and honest discernment process that leads to the communal learning that itself is an essential part of the growth of a true community of faith.

Another important resource on the nature of the Christian community of faith is a book by Dietrich Bonhoeffer, a well-known German Protestant minister, written in 1938, four years before he was arrested by the Nazi Gestapo for his involvement in a plot to assassinate Adolf Hitler. He was executed by special order of Heinrich Himmler just before the prison camp where he was being held was liberated by the Allies toward the end of World War II. The book, entitled *Life Together,* is a treatise on the Christian community from a Lutheran perspective. As such, it offers some interesting commentary on such topics as confession, ministry, prayer, fellowship, and love of one's neighbor. In it, Bonhoeffer makes this observation:

> In a Christian community everything depends upon whether each individual is an indispensable link in the chain. Only when even the smallest link is securely interlocked is the chain unbreakable.[49]

What he is saying is that *we all matter.* He is asserting not only that we are indispensable, but that we must also *believe* we are indispensable. My point here is that the learning process involves accessing a wide range of resources not only about our faith, but also about the complex process of community building. Learning about each other, learning about

49 Dietrich Bonhoeffer, *Life Together* (New York: Harper & Row, 1954), 94.

Jesus Christ, and learning about how to be in community are all fundamentals of being an authentic Christian community of faith.

DIALOGUE TOGETHER

While our Protestant traditions were from the beginning based on an empowerment of the laity, in the Catholic tradition Vatican II lent a new vigor to the Catholic Church's understanding of the role of the laity and particularly the necessity for healthy dialogue within the Christian community of faith. The following two quotations capture some of that spirit. The first is from The Decree on the Apostolate of the Lay People:

> The parish offers an outstanding example of community apostolate, for it gathers into a unity all the human diversities that are found there and inserts them into the universality of the Church. The laity should develop the habit of working in the parish in close union with their priests, of bringing before the ecclesial community their own problems, world problems and questions regarding man's salvation, to examine them together and solve them by general discussion.[50]

Also, in The Pastoral Constitution on the Church in the Modern World:

> Very often their Christian vision will suggest a certain solution in some given situation. Yet it

50 Second Vatican Ecumenical Council, Decree on the Apostolate of the Lay People, *Apostolicam Actuositatem*, section 10.

happens rather frequently, and legitimately so, that some of the faithful, with no less sincerity, will see the problem quite differently. Now if one or other of the proposed solutions is too easily associated with the message of the Gospel, they ought to remember that in those cases no one is permitted to identify the authority of the Church exclusively with his own opinion. Let them try to guide each other by sincere dialogue in a spirit of mutual charity and with anxious interest above all in the common good.

The laity are called to participate actively in the whole life of the Church, not only are they to animate the world with the spirit of Christianity, but they are to be witnesses to Christ in all circumstances and at the very heart of the community of mankind.[51]

The conclusion one should draw from this guidance is that both clergy and laity should be in open and charitable dialogue concerning the meaning of the deposit of faith and how that meaning can and should be manifest in the community's internal relationships and external ministries. Protestants may take much of this for granted, but for Catholics, the call to dialogue within the community is a departure from the perceived authoritarian structure, which has formed the basis of much of the Catholic life in the not-so-distant past.

While we might conclude that dialogue is important, we

---

51 Second Vatican Ecumenical Council, The Pastoral Constitution of the Church in the Modern World, *Gaudium et Spes*, section 43.

often think of dialogue as synonymous with the term *discussion*. Although this might be true in many instances, Joseph Ratzinger (Pope Benedict XVI) points out a stunning truth concerning the nature of dialogue within the community of faith.

> No real dialogue yet takes place where men are still only talking about *something*. The conversation between men comes into its own only when they are trying, no longer to express something, but to express themselves, when dialogue becomes communication . . . That is why the testimony of God is inaudible where language is no more than a technique for imparting "something." God does not occur in logistic calculations. Perhaps the difficulty we find today in speaking about God arises precisely from the very fact that our language is tending more and more to become pure calculation, that it is becoming more and more a mere means of passing on technical information, less and less a means for our common being to make contact in the *logos* [the living Word of God], a process in which intuitively or deliberately contact is also made with the ground of all things.[52]

This distinction between talking about *something* and *sharing* oneself is indeed a subtle one, and yet if we look at discussions we often have about doctrine or the meaning of Scripture, it is easy to see how such discussions devolve into an

---

52 Joseph Cardinal Ratzinger, *Introduction to Christianity* (2d ed.; San Francisco: Ignatius Press, 2004), 95–6.

exchange of ideas without any creativity. I tell you what I think, you tell me what you think, and that is it. Our mode of discussion often takes the form of poker betting. I make this bet based on the cards in my hand, and you may check, call, raise, or fold based on the cards in your hand, but our cards remain hidden and exclusively our own. The competitive nature of poker and the goal of winning the pot would ludicrously break down if those of us around the table began to enter into dialogue about the cards we held—but that is precisely what we are suggesting concerning our dialogue in the community of faith. This dialogue is tantamount to putting all the poker hands on the table and together trying to build the best possible hand with no winners or losers. Unfortunately, our "dialogue" often looks like a series of monologues with the best one taking the pot.

But what if we were all searching for a truth larger than any one of us has alone? What would it look like if you told me what you think, and I take what you have said and build on it, adding my own spin to help fill out the idea further, while someone else adds something of their own? The result would be something *new*. By not only offering our ideas, but also *ourselves* as open vessels in search of the truth, we participate in the creativity of God. In fact, by our very openness we have allowed God to participate in our dialogue. We would say that the Holy Spirit had a seat at the table.

The posture of openness to the truth is nothing less than being a good thinker. Scientists who are not open are not good scientists. Writers who are not open probably cannot write much of any value that is new. Politicians who are closed to the truth, at least we would hope, eventually would be discovered as frauds and voted out of office. If we are clothed in our own narrow thoughts and unable to "accessorize" ourselves with the valid thoughts of others, we may be standing there in shreds that effectively reveal that we "have no real clothes on at all." In the end, we are intellectually and spiritually naked—stripped of meaning that derives from a context that is larger than ourselves.

Real dialogue requires transparency, transparency requires a willingness to risk, a willingness to risk requires trust, and trust requires love. We therefore have no real dialogue without love. In fact, dialogue looks and feels very different among those who know and love each other. There is a delight in the mutual search for the truth, because when it is found everyone is enriched. Even someone outside looking in should recognize the precious rarity of dialogue between those who love. In other words, one might say that the *search* for the truth in love *is* the pearl of great price. It is life itself. To the degree that the Holy Spirit has a seat at the table, true dialogue is a participation in *life eternal*—the life of God.

PRACTICE TOGETHER

One never knows whether one has learned anything until one is called upon to put it into practice. The community of faith is designed to be a place where we can practice our faith in a setting of trust. This requirement of trust is so important that we should dwell here for a moment. To step out as Christ in the world is a daunting challenge. Many would have us believe that if we were *all* Christ-like, everything would be rosy, and that probably is true. The problem comes in the intermediate stages where only a few are trying to be Christ-like in an environment dominated by those who have no understanding of what we are about. Sometimes there is nothing funnier than someone trying to think and act like Jesus. We had better have a good sense of humor, because we certainly will mess it up as we gird up our courage and step out in faith. We may look foolish if we think God is telling us to "raise Grandma from the dead" when he actually wants us to "praise Grandma for the bread." This is why trust in the community of faith is so essential. One must trust that all present understand the challenges and fears and mistakes that need to be overcome in order for us to step out as Christ in the world. But step out in faith we must—no matter how potentially silly it may make us look to others. This is why we need a safe place to *practice*.

The community of faith is therefore a place of trust in which all can practice the many aspects of "being" Christ in the world—all the way from the kindness Jesus had with little children to the boldness he demonstrated as he confronted the Pharisees, from showing the same trust and confidence in the Father that Christ did when he prayed, to having the same trust and confidence to suffer ridicule for standing in the truth as Christ did when he stood in and reflected the truth of the Father. We must practice all of these. Being like Jesus is not easy, and it takes time and practice even to begin to understand who he was, what he went through, and how to live into the life he calls us into.

Finally, the community of faith is the place to integrate all the many parts of the Christian mystery around the central organizing principles of love and our transformation into the perfect likeness of Jesus Christ. There are thousands of these parts that we encounter during our lives as Christians. The *Imitation of Christ* by Thomas à Kempis is a veritable litany of virtues that the Christian should strive to integrate into his or her life.[53] They include humility, prudence, self-control,

---

53 Thomas à Kempis, *The Imitation of Christ* (New York: Penguin Classics, 1952).

obedience, peace, suffering, patience, contrition, meditation, righteousness, courage, temperance, justice, chastity, charity, diligence, kindness, and on and on. Without the organizing principle of love, the effort to satisfy the list would drive us to insanity. Without the enabling faith in Jesus Christ, the satisfaction of the demands of the list would be impossible. With both love and faith, however, we are assured that eternal life has been made available to us right here and now—and with that life comes humility, prudence, self-control, etc. But there must be one place where we are challenged and encouraged to fit the pieces together, to see what they mean and put them into practice. This is the role of the community of faith.

PRAY TOGETHER

A vital prayer life is so integral to all of the components of a Christian community that it is not at all clear where it should be placed in the list. Certainly we *learn* to pray. But just as certainly we pray to *learn*. One's heart and mind cannot be opened to the knowledge that the Holy Spirit wants to bestow on us without being open to that Spirit. Likewise the *practice* of prayer (finding the time and place, assuming a prayerful posture) in some way precedes the prayer itself, while prayer conditions all *practice*. Everything leads to prayer and prayer leads to everything. Thus, a rich prayer experience is an essential component of a legitimate community of faith.

One of the great contributions of the Protestant traditions as well as the charismatic movement is the idea of extemporaneous prayer. While many of us grow up using the prayers in the Episcopal *Book of Common Prayer* or any one of several Catholic missals, we often are limited to these prayers. In other words, we really do not know how to pray. When Jesus was asked to show the disciples how to pray, he did not go to a book and look up the Lord's Prayer. His prayer was from a heart totally open to the movement of the Holy Spirit. In other words, it was extemporaneous. One of the challenges for those of us from a more liturgical background is to learn how to allow the Holy Spirit to pray *through us*. The community of faith can have two essential functions: to model prayer in the lives of those who have learned to pray and to create a safe place for the rest of us to practice prayer. We may start out with anxiety and self-consciousness at first, but gradually we feel more comfortable with the open-endedness of our prayer. We are not praying to the group. We are praying to God and allowing the group to sit in. This prayer thus becomes an edifying blessing to all those present. As long as we are dependent on the prayers of others as a crutch, however, the Holy Spirit will be limited in our lives and the lives of the community of faith. This does not mean that liturgy, the Lord's Prayer, the prayers of Saint Ignatius or Martin Luther, are not of great value. The repetition of well-known prayers has its own power to unlock the prayers in our own heart, but at some point we all must learn to step beyond them in faith and trust that God can help us to pray from the heart for our benefit and the benefit and edification of our respective communities of faith.

PLAY TOGETHER

Now this one is possibly the most unobvious and yet most important characteristic of a community of faith. The degree to which we take ourselves too seriously[54] (we might call

---

54 One of the most famous quotations from Teresa of Avila is, "Take God very seriously; but don't take yourself seriously at all."

this *pride*) is precisely the degree to which we cut ourselves off from the larger truth that flows from God. We certainly are called to take Christ seriously and to take our journey seriously, but along the way we cannot but chuckle at our own massive failure to fulfill the possibilities that have been offered to us. As I said, there is often nothing funnier than a bunch of folks running around trying to *be* Jesus. We see through a mirror dimly and our hearing is impaired by the background noise of our own woundedness. If we do not carry with us a considerable sense of humor, we are destined to implode on our own failures.

While being able to laugh at ourselves is an essential component of our journey toward Christ, it is also true in a real trusting community of faith that we can laugh *with* each other *about* each other. I grew up with the adage of my father as he was chuckling at something I might have done: "I'm not laughing *at* you, I am laughing *with* you." I used to be both frustrated and angry at this remark, because *I was not laughing.* I think the point of this is that to a large extent we control whether or not someone is laughing at us or laughing with us. If we easily laugh at our own expense, then others, especially those we trust, are always laughing with us. Now that does not preclude those with wounded self-images to laugh at others in order to build themselves up. Sometimes these folks just need to see the model of a community of faith laughing about each other in order to see the value of this alternative.

So play is the ability to be playful with each other. It is not essentially about playing cards or soccer, or even going to the movies, sporting events or concerts together, although these kinds of play can lead to the deeper playfulness I am talking about. Unfortunately, playing games such as chess, monopoly, tennis, or football often involves a level of self-centered competitiveness that overpowers its potential for true playfulness. It may be fun to beat the tar out of your opponent and to work with your teammates to do it, but it is a pale reflection of the kind of play that is possible and desirable in the community of faith. What we are talking about here is more like the play of children who have no competitive goal other than just play. You can see this as they set up a fort and move their trucks and plastic soldiers around with abandon. Adults can do this as they move the pieces of their lives around with abandon in order to engage each other just for the sake of the relationship itself, without any ulterior motive or long-term goal. Sometimes we see this kind of play when families are working together to prepare Thanksgiving dinner or decorating the Christmas tree.

Formal play, however, can be done with or without playfulness and may or may not add to the community-building experience. When I was an Episcopalian in Columbia, South Carolina, once a year we would have a church picnic at Camp Gravatt. Inevitably, we would have a volleyball game. It would start out as a bunch of individuals on either side of the net trying to return the ball to the other side of the net—until we instituted a rule: each team had to touch the ball three times before it could be returned. It was almost miraculous how the connectedness and joy accompanied this new need for each other. Games and other group activities, if done in the right way, can go far in enhancing the connectedness and playfulness of the community of faith.

C. S. Lewis makes an insightful comment, however, about the dangers of play that is worth noting.[55] While trust can yield an unusual amount of honesty and "ribbing" from

---

55 Lewis, *Surprised by Joy* and *The Four Loves*, 251.

friends, the protocol associated with that kind of play is very subtle and should be very precise. Knowing when and how to kid someone about themselves only arises from time together and sensitivity. Many are hurt by a crude and insensitive kind of play that is unworthy of the high level of transparency that is earned over time in a community of faith. So, strive for a high level of play, but be sensitive to its natural limits that only are expanded with time and a growing familiarity and trust.

ACCOUNTABILITY TOWARD ONE ANOTHER

The idea that we should be accountable toward one another arises out of our natural interconnectedness. If indeed life is all about relationships, then we cannot exist in a vacuum. Our actions affect others and other's actions affect us, even if we may not see the cause and effect manifest in concrete and obvious ways. We might say that it is a statement of faith rather than a statement of scientific empirical analysis. If we are inherently interconnected, whether we like it or not, then we have a responsibility toward one another. I have a responsibility to drive safely so that I do not put others at risk. I have a responsibility not to engage in immoral behavior so that I do not use others in a less-than-fully-human manner or lead others into such behavior. I have a responsibility to be consistent with my participation in the community of faith, because others depend on me as I depend on them. In other words, we are accountable to each other.

We should expect that part of our dialogue with each other will be about how we are doing in our obligations to each other. If we have made a commitment, we should be expected to keep it. We are so often disappointed by folks failing to fulfill their commitments that we no longer have any expectations that they will be fulfilled in the future. This kind of cynicism infects our whole society, probably because we have no community to which we belong that has fostered an abiding and steadfast trust on which we can depend. The community of faith should have as one of its central purposes the development of trust, and that cannot be accomplished if no one is willing to make a commitment and keep it. But this is not only true in the community of faith. While it should be a "proving ground" for trust-building, the community of faith should also be a "nursery" for the growing of trust and integrity in other areas of our lives. Doing what we say we are going to do is a fundamental virtue in school, business, society, and politics. People you cannot trust soon get left by the wayside. The community of faith can be a powerful training ground for habits of making and fulfilling commitments. The discussion of how we are doing in this area would come under the heading of *accountability*.

One other theme that might be included under this heading is the question posed by Cain in the book of Genesis. After Cain has killed his brother Abel, God asks Cain where his brother is. Cain responds that he does not know, polishing off the exchange with, "Am I my brother's keeper" (Gen 4:9)? Now, the answer is never explicitly given, but we can be pretty sure that the answer is "Yes, you are your brother's keeper, and you have a responsibility for his welfare." This kind of pervasive responsibility for each other is precisely what we are placing under the topic of accountability. If we fail to pay attention to the needs of others, if we fail to respond to the needs of others, and if we fail to hold each other accountable for those failures, we are functioning as did Cain.

We must, however, note that our active "concern" for

others can be a huge self-serving, ego-building trap. It is critical that we place our desires to interject ourselves into the lives of others to some form of test. Who is being served here? All too often we allow our own self-satisfaction to overwhelm our better judgment—or more specifically the will of God—as we barge in "where angels fear to tread," making a mess of a difficult and complex situation that we did not fully understand. The opposite may also be true— that we have acted in good faith and have been misinterpreted. In each of these cases we may be called to begin an action only to be called to put the bus in reverse and quickly back it out. The problem we are addressing here is our ability to know and act on the truth and will of God. We call this discernment, and it is clearly an essential aspect of our understanding of accountability within the community of faith.

DISCERNMENT TOGETHER

Before we explore the way in which discernment can take place within a community of faith, we should make a distinction that is often missed between *discernment* and *judgment*. We are using the word discernment to mean recognizing a difference or making a distinction—just as we are doing with these two words. It may be as simple as discerning if the stoplight is red, or more challenging, as discerning if your spouse is having an affair. Each case involves a process of paying attention and making a distinction between a red light and a green light or a spousal relationship that is quirky and one that is solid. While we are not called to *judge*, we certainly are called to *discern*. What is the difference? As we said, the process of discernment is simply one of figuring out what is true. The process of judgment, at least in the biblical sense, is one of assigning value. If I discern that my friend is an alcoholic and initiate an intervention, this is a good thing and is a responsibility I have to my "brother." If I gloat over the idea that I am better than he is, this is a kind of judgment that is not available to one who calls himself a Christian. If in my anger I assert that someone is going to hell for their actions, I am involved in the act of judgment—and we believe only God can do that. If I discern that someone has engaged in heinous actions by murdering one or more people, I may be involved in a judicial process that results in that person spending the rest of their natural life in prison. Assigning consequences to actions does not necessarily involve a judgment as to that person's worth in the eyes of God.

As we mentioned above, the problem of individual discernment, especially when it involves others, is an age-old problem. We could say that the problem of discerning the will of God is the oldest challenge to Christians—or to any person of any faith, for that matter. Jesus in the Garden of Gethsemane was himself in a process of discernment. The apostles were continually in a process of discernment as to the nature of Jesus, Paul was in a process of discernment on the road to Damascus, and all the rest of us are in a process of discernment when seeking the will of God for our lives. In fact, we could assume that when Paul admonishes us to pray ceaselessly,[56] he is saying for us to be in a posture of prayerful discernment at all times.

In this context, we find some powerful traditions in the Church that focus on individual discernment.[57] Ignatius of

---

56 1 Thess 5:17.
57 For this discussion of both individual and communal discernment, I have drawn from a wonderful paper by Bruce Bishop, entitled "Comparison of Discernment in the Early Jesuit and Quaker Communities," which can be found at http://nwfriends.org/media/Jesuit_and_Quaker_disc.pdf.

Loyola, in his *Spiritual Exercises,* explicitly addressed the challenge, offering a concrete process that involved paying attention to what he called "consolations" and "desolations"—interior responses to issues of discernment. This process of perceiving, through further meditation and rational evaluation, leads to an understanding that forms the basis of action. The tests of a valid discernment are its relationship to the service and glory of God, to the salvation of the soul, to a basis in Scripture, to its leading to our likeness to Christ, to a feeling of peace or consolation, and finally, to a rational evaluation of its merit relative to other alternatives.[58]

One of the most important aspects of Ignatian discernment is the posture of detachment from all things of this world. Any perception is tainted by our attachments to things, people, and outcomes. For us to be in a correct posture of discernment we must be so indifferent to the outcome that we are perfectly supple in the "hands" of God.

Finally, any conclusion regarding discernment must be offered to God for confirmation. This is not a one-shot deal of checking in with God, getting our ticket punched, and then moving forward with vigor, conviction, and blinders. It is a process of holding the conclusion gingerly in our grasp and continuing to pay attention to the promptings of the Holy Spirit, in case the confirmation is falsely interpreted or is removed. In other words, we are not even to be attached to what we believe God is confirming. As we mentioned above, we are always confronted by the fact that we see through a mirror dimly and hear with impaired acuity.

Now, up to this point we have been talking about individual personal discernment, but what about discernment in

---

58 Ignatius of Loyola, *The Spiritual Exercises of Saint Ignatius* (trans. Anthony Mottola; New York: Image Books, 1964) 129–34.

community? For this topic we should turn to the Quakers, for the discernment of the will of God in community is a central purpose of their very life. George Fox in his journal described how discernment played a major role in his spiritual way of life.[59] Like Ignatius, Fox offered a number of norms by which he judged the validity of discernment. These included: that it was "of the Cross" or contrary to one's self-will, agreeable to Scripture, invoked the presence of inner peace, and was consistent with the revelation to others. This last norm is of particular interest to us in our discussion of discernment in the context of the community of faith. Fox and the entire Quaker tradition that followed his lead saw an indispensable value in the testing of one's discernment within the community.[60] Because we "see through a mirror dimly," our personal vision is always a bit fuzzy. It is only through the eyes of others in our community of faith that we are offered the possibility of a clearer vision. In fact, we could see this same clarification showing up as we experience, enter into dialogue, learn, pray, and play together. Just as the Holy Spirit is acting through us to bring us wisdom and understanding, the Holy Spirit is acting through others in our own community of faith to inform our own experience of the Holy Spirit. We really cannot do it alone, but always in relationship with others.

Now, this communal discernment has its limits. If we are in a position of being bold concerning a problem or issue that we feel needs to be addressed, it is all too easy for us to be dismissed because we have not gotten the confirmation of the rest of the community of faith. The problem with

---

59 George Fox, *The Journal of George Fox* (ed. Norman Penney, New York: Cosimo, 2007).

60 Bishop, 6. (See note 56 above.)

this absolute norm is that sometimes God *does* speak to us as individuals and asks us to step out in faith in the midst of complete opposition, to take a stand, or press ahead with an agenda that may seem to others to be our own but may in fact be God's agenda. The history of the prophets and saints is replete with examples of individuals who "bucked the system." Starting with Isaiah, Jeremiah, Jesus Christ himself and following with St. Francis of Assisi, St. Teresa of Avila, and St. Maximus the Confessor, all prophets and saints ran up against opposition somewhere. If there had been no *status quo*—that which was "tried and true"—there would have been no opposition. Unfortunately, the model for our lives, Jesus Christ, turned the *status quo* on its head, and we should not be surprised that Jesus' followers would at some point do the same within their local environments.

In this context, we have a bit of a dilemma. When do we trust our own personal discernment and when do we trust the confirmation of our community of faith? Both Ignatius and Fox offer invaluable guidelines for the process of arriving at an action that is the result of discerning the true will of God. Having a legitimate community of faith with which to share and discuss our thoughts is an essential part of our active journey toward Christ. The literature is ample that can help in this process. The central norm that gets unfolded within the community of faith is the love of Christ. As long as we are rooted in this ultimate norm, we will be starting from the right perspective. How that love works itself out in our lives is the object of our continual discernment with the aid of the Holy Spirit in the context of an authentic Christian community of faith.

MINISTER TO OTHERS

So often we think of ministries as those toward others outside our communities of faith: the homeless, the sick, the lost, the afflicted, and the confused. Often what we fail to see is that ministry starts at home. If we cannot minister to those with whom we are in relationship within our own communities of faith, how do we expect our ministries to others outside our communities of faith to be meaningful? We can certainly be kept busy, and we can feel the satisfaction of helping others, but until we see the subtle opportunities for ministry that unfold all around us within our own communities of faith, we cannot be tuned into the depth of opportunities that unfold in our ministries to others outside those communities. So we must start at home. Ministering to others begins with *paying attention*—noticing what is going on around us. When you come and go from worship, look up and greet those you encounter. When you ask, "How are you today?" mean it and see if someone is willing actually to tell you. Be prepared to stop and share the love of Christ. Here is an interesting twist. If someone asks *you*, "How are you today?" You might test the waters by starting actually to tell them. If they pause to hear what you are saying, you have found an opportunity for both of you to minister to one another. Ministry is not just giving. We pounce on the adage, "It is more blessed to give than to receive," but that is not necessarily always true. Sometimes it is more blessed to receive that which others have to give than simply to be giving all the time and being unable to receive. As Joseph Ratzinger observed: "Indeed, we must put it more pointedly: hell consists in man's being unwilling to receive anything."[61]

Sometimes giving is just a way to hide, because receiving

---

61 Ratzinger, *Introduction to Christianity,* 239.

makes us uncomfortable—even vulnerable—and places us in someone's debt. Receiving may often be the most precious gift we can offer. One of the reasons we have so much trouble being Christ-like with others is that *they will have none of it*. They are unable or unwilling to receive that Christ-likeness. It is not so much that *we* are unable or unwilling to offer it, but others are unable or unwilling to *receive* it. It is only when we are *equally* willing to give *and* receive within the community of faith that we are ready to step outside that community and offer authentic ministry to others.

Now here is a basic limitation to the idea that we can and need to prepare ourselves within the community of faith for ministry to others outside it. Cynthia de Berry Freeman once said, "God has to use us and shape us up, all at the same time."[62] I don't know whether she originated the thought or not, but it is a good one. We cannot expect to be perfected before we step out as instruments of God's love and grace. What we should keep in mind is that, as our own lives are continually perfected, so will our ministry to others. What we cannot do is substitute those ministries for our own spiritual growth within the community of faith. If we do, those ministries simply become a distraction to the fundamental transformation into the perfect likeness of Jesus Christ that is the cornerstone of our Christian purpose. As that transformation progresses, it will push and drag us into a life of giving to others both within and outside our communities of faith. We will gradually *become* a gift—in all the fullness that the word "gift" might imply.

---

62 Personal communication in an oral sermon.

* * *

All these functions of an authentic Christian community of faith and the way they work together, what we have been calling the "fit" of the community, have an essential purpose—to deepen relationships and allow them to exhibit the love of Christ. While they can to some extent be orchestrated, the results of that effort clearly have to do with the degree to which the Holy Spirit is allowed to mold these relationships and the individuals that enter into them. What flows outward from that community, what we are calling the "feel" and "finish" can also be understood as the *fruits* of that community.

17

THE "FEEL" OF CHRISTIAN COMMUNITY

We have been talking about the fit of the community of faith—the way the functional parts fit together, and how they work. But what is the *feel* of the community if all the parts are working—if they fit together and function as they are intended? We could say that the "feel" of the community of faith is how it "feels"—both to its participants and to those who might be observing it from the outside. We might be entering into some form of dialogue, but the *feel* of that dialogue is one of patience, humility, and self-control. We may be holding each other accountable, but the *feel* is one of gentleness, kindness, and a lack of judgmentalism. What might *feel* like an argument to some could have the *feel* of a vigorous and delightful search for the truth—together—to others. The *feel* is deeper and less easy to nail down than are the more functional characteristics, and yet it is this *feel* that lets everyone know that what they are experiencing is something much more than an intellectual discussion group or an informative Bible study.

The feel of the community of faith is much more abstract and difficult to articulate, let alone orchestrate. Basically it comes from the heart, and that means it is conditioned by the activity of the Holy Spirit. Our first problem is that no one exactly knows what the heart really is. Clearly, it is not merely the cardio-vascular pump in the middle of the chest, although for some reason it seems to reside in that region. There is a physical correlation between the place of the physical heart and the place that is affected when we talk of something being "heartwarming." All we can assert is that the spiritual heart is a mystery related to the image of God with which we were endowed at our creation. It has to do with our *soul*.

Now, since the heart is a bit of a mystery, one can see that those characteristics of the community of faith that are related to the heart themselves are a bit mysterious. It is hard to nail them down. With that caveat in mind, let's try to point out a few of the characteristics. Some of the ones that come to mind are: honesty, patience, compassion, suffering, joy, purity, chastity, constancy, faith, hope, and charity (that would be love). These are the virtues—the same things Thomas à Kempis wrote about in *The Imitation of Christ*,[63] and Paul stresses in his letters to the Gentile Christian communities, known as the *fruit of the Spirit*:

> But the fruit of the Spirit is love, joy, peace, patience, kindness, goodness, faithfulness, self-control. (Gal 5:22–23)

---

63 Thomas à Kempis, *The Imitation of Christ* (London: Penguin Books, 1952).

While dialogue, experience, prayer, and play can help us on our journey, the ultimate point of the journey is the "feel" of the community of faith—the way it actually works to grow us spiritually and the way it works itself out in our relationships with others. What follows are a few of the characteristics of an authentic community of faith that spring from a "functioning" community. While most of these characteristics have been mentioned before, it is useful here to focus on them as a class apart from the functions or "fit" of the community. What we will see from the following brief discussions is that all of these characteristics overlap. It is almost impossible to talk about one without recognizing its foundation in the others. These are not mutually independent characteristics, but are more like one characteristic—love—viewed from a number of different vantage points.

BELONGING

Through sharing, dialogue, play, and ministry we break through the shields that tend to protect us from the harm that can come to us from openness and vulnerability. We start to feel that we belong—not just because we have some form of credentials such as being a card-carrying Episcopalian, Methodist, or Catholic, or a member of AARP, NRA, ACLU, or Sam's Club, but because we are recognized and accepted for who we really are. We need no disguise or pretense. We gradually start to operate on the foundational assumption that we are an integral part of something and that the something would be the poorer were we not there. As we mentioned above, we all want to be where everybody knows our name. But more than that, we want to be where everyone sees through our façade and values the unique characteristics that we bring to the table.

ACCEPTANCE

One of the critical aspects of belonging is acceptance. It is not that we serve up what others expect us to be. It is not that we are always likable or agreeable or even tolerable according to some outside measurement. It is that who we really are is accepted with all our flaws and blemishes. This is so much more than being tolerated. We are loved precisely because we are real and accessible to those around us. To be accepted in this way is to be loved and not judged. Now that does not mean that others are not fully aware of our shortcomings. In fact they are more aware of them than anyone else. This awareness arises specifically from the level of interaction within the community. It arises from sharing, dialogue, play and ministry. It flows from a gradual chipping away of barriers. To be accepted in this way is to be seen clearly and understood deeply. The one characteristic that drives this kind of acceptance is compassion.

COMPASSION

The compassion that develops from a deep openness in community is simply the ability of participants to look below the surface of another's external limitations and flaws in order to see the same brokenness and vulnerability we all share. We would have to assert that this kind of compassion was most fully developed in Jesus Christ himself. So while we may be stressing the love of Christ, we could just as well be talking about the *compassion of Christ*—a compassion that goes far beyond what most of us practice on a day-to-day basis. And yet it is precisely this capacity that we are trying to foster within the community of faith. The only way we can do this is by coming back together consistently to chip away at the façade that we all erect for our personal protection. In other words, we learn this kind of compassion as we grow in our sense of belonging, acceptance, and trust.

TRUST

We could have placed trust at the top of the list as a starting point or we could start to see it as a result of the development of other characteristics. In any event, trust is central to the process of developing meaningful sharing, dialogue, and especially play. We might assert that there is no real sharing, dialogue, or play without trust. In fact, the way we know that people trust each other is the way they look when they enter into these ways of relating to one another. And yet trust is not easily achieved. It requires a willingness to be vulnerable—an exposure that makes it possible for us to be hurt. Consequently, it takes time for a group of people to grow into a trusting community. Some have such strong barriers that have grown out of such deep wounds that trust is impossible. While acceptance and compassion can be one-sided and are always possible, trust is something that is mutually shared and is yielded gradually by those in relationship. And yet it is only through the yielding of mutual trust that the depth of community can be achieved. This yielding of trust is effectively the same thing as a yielding of self—a removal of our false front—a development of transparency.

TRANSPARENCY

As should be clear, belonging, acceptance, compassion, and trust all are predicated on some level of transparency. We might say that transparency is best captured by the phrase, "What you see is what you get—and I offer it all to you." The ability to be real and transparent with everyone we meet is a daunting challenge, and yet we might assert that Jesus offered precisely this kind of openness. He hid nothing and offered all of himself to those he encountered. The difficulty we have in offering this kind of transparency is precisely why we need to work at it in a trusting environment. But we also must realize that as we develop this characteristic, the light of love and truth that accompanies this level of gift-of-self, the light of Christ, begins to shine outward from the community of faith and attracts others to enter this way of transformation.

OTHER-CENTEREDNESS

While transparency is something that we can exhibit without much concern for others, a natural extension of this gift-of-self is a concern for others. By offering ourselves to others we begin to see this concern for others not as a nice addition or even a part of the Eleventh Commandment, but an essential part of who we are as human beings. Just as Paul admonishes us to assume a prayerful posture at all times, Jesus implicitly admonishes us to center our lives on others *at all times*. This other-centeredness becomes an integral part of who we are—how our heart beats, how we breathe, and what we do with our mind, body, and spirit. To be changed into an other-centered person is to be transformed into the perfect likeness of Jesus Christ, and it is in the community of faith that we learn how to do this—or at least allow the Holy Spirit to invade us in such a way that we become this new person in Christ.

This movement of the Holy Spirit into our very being, setting up shop, taking over, and running the whole show only happens as we break down the barrier of self-centeredness. This process has for centuries been known as a pathway away from *attachment* and toward *detachment*.

DETACHMENT

All the mystics talk of the problem of *attachment* and the way it keeps us from being totally supple in the "hands" of God. This can involve attachment to things like houses, cars, money, attachment to individuals like spouses, children or friends, or inordinate attachment to self—one's ego. All of the functions of the community of faith are disrupted by attachments. It is only when we start letting go of these attachments that the functions start to work freely and the fruits start to flow forth. Becoming detached does not mean that we don't care. It just means that we are willing for God to operate without our interference. We strive to be instruments without being directors. Again, achieving or allowing this kind of detachment is not easy and runs counter to much of our modern culture, but that is the deal—and the community of faith is the place to seek this overarching virtue.

GRACE~FILLED

When the angel Gabriel comes to Mary to announce the birth of Jesus, he says "Hail, full of grace."[64] The idea is so strong that, irrespective of one's translational bias, we ourselves need to come to terms with the idea of being *filled with grace*. Clearly the Catholic Church has taken it to mean that Mary was without sin, but what about us? What might being filled with grace mean for us, how might it take place, and what would we look like if we were thus filled? The word "graceful" immediately comes to mind implying a lack of roughness—a fluid movement that exhibits a level of comfort

---

64 Luke 1:28. This is often translated "highly favored one," but my point loses some of its oomph if I go in that direction.

and security. The word "gracious" also captures some important characteristics that include a natural generosity and a cognizance of the needs of others. In other words, one who is filled with the grace of God is one who has received and offered to others the free gift of what God has *provided* to his children—his providence. This gift would include not only the gifts of the Spirit as articulated by Paul, such as wisdom, knowledge, faith, and healing (1 Cor 12:1–11), but must also include the fruit of the Spirit such as love, joy, peace, forbearance, kindness, goodness, faithfulness, gentleness, and self-control (Gal 5:22–23). Since the one who exhibited all these characteristics to the extent possible for a human being was Jesus Christ, to be grace-filled is to be transformed into the likeness of Jesus Christ. Our thesis here is that it is only through the community of faith that one has an opportunity to develop these characteristics that exhibit the love of Christ among members and shine forth as a sign of Christ's love.

DELIGHT

We have talked about play as one of the functions of the community of faith. What is interesting about the ability to play is that it is predicated on a certain level of trust. We know what play looks like when we see it, but it is not so clear how to orchestrate it. One of the tell-tale signs that play is taking place, however, is the presence of delight among the participants. We have said that we are not called to take ourselves too seriously even though we take our journey toward Christ seriously. This delight in our own limitations is a critical aspect of humility which itself is a critical aspect of play. Our delight in the unique characteristics, abilities, and accomplishments of others is also a hallmark of play. This delight should be immensely attractive to those who are looking on from the outside.

Now, we have all seen movies where a boy and girl are frolicking across the college quadrangle tackling each other and making angels in the snow. I don't know about you, but it all seems a bit artificial to me. Maybe the reason is that it requires no real intimacy—no delight in our own transparency. The kind of delight we are alluding to here is one that is based on this deeper kind of openness and trust. It doesn't happen overnight, but only with a committed repeated return to the process of community building—even if it is only a community of two. In some way, it is related to our openness to being filled with the Spirit of love and truth—the Holy Spirit.

SPIRIT-FILLED

The concept of being *Spirit-filled* has been approached from many different directions recently. Many renewal movements profess to open participants to the activity of the Holy Spirit. The charismatic movement emphasizes the activity of the Holy Spirit in prayer and worship. Some feel uncomfortable with what appears to be a loosening of our emotional restraints. Resting in the Spirit is therefore looked upon with suspicion. On the other hand, the New Testament is full of allusions to the activity of the Holy Spirit. Believing Christians cannot ignore the event of Pentecost. We would like to know what the expected activity of the Holy Spirit should look like in a normal, average-every-day, run-of-the-mill, Spirit-filled community of faith that Jesus would recognize as flowing naturally out of his saving mission. For an answer, we might look at the activity of prayer. Everyone should agree that prayer is a fundamental function of the community of faith. As we become more and more a praying community, we might ask whether the nature of that prayer evolves into something that is more Spirit-filled. The answer of course is—uh, well, *of course*. Just as the apostles asked Jesus to teach them how to pray, we as members of an authentic community of faith will gradually learn how to pray more and more deeply. In other words, our prayers will be less and less an intellectual exercise whereby we recite memorized prayers or read prayers that were written by others, and will be more and more an activity of the Holy Spirit. We will not only become more and more open to the movement of the Spirit in our prayer, but in our whole lives. We will become more and more *Spirit-filled*.

If this is so, is there a point in which we start to look different from those around us who are not on this journey? The answer is, probably so, but the difference may not be so radical as to put people off. If we are sensitive to where others are on their respective journeys, we probably will not break out in tongues at the drop of a hat, because this would be a stumbling block to those who do not understand what is going on. In other settings we might just find that resting in the Spirit and praying in the Spirit (speaking in tongues) are the most normal ways of expressing the fact that we feel filled by the Spirit of God—overwhelmed by the love of Christ that has filled us to overflowing.

Our life in the Spirit is a journey of deepening openness. We should not expect it to take off quickly if it is to be well-grounded. If it does take off quickly, we might take care that we are not indulging in an emotional high that may or may not have anything to do with the activity of the Holy Spirit. On the other hand, we should expect that our life in an authentic Christian community of faith should become more and more Spirit-filled—which is the same thing as saying that it should become more and more filled with the love of Christ.

LOVE

Earlier we went to considerable lengths to talk about the wide range of definitions of the word "love." As we grow in our understanding of the love of Christ, which of course is the love of God, we deepen our appreciation that this love encompasses many of the characteristics we have been talking about: transparency, acceptance, compassion, delight, trust, and the presence of God's grace and Spirit. This love of Christ is not so easy to nail down, but at least we can talk about the other kinds of love that are more limited such as *eros, storge,* and *philia. Agape,* or the love of God, has as its object always the good of the other, and it is this selfless love that should grow in the community of faith. It is this free gift that is offered with no strings attached that should start to flower as members share, dialogue, and enter into transparent play.

This love has an interesting characteristic: it is founded upon the same acts of giving, receiving, and returning that are reflected in the very nature of God. It is founded on the relationship between the three Persons of the Holy Trinity: the Father, Son, and Holy Spirit. In other words, the love that is being acted out in the community of faith is the same love that is being acted out in the very nature of God. This giving, receiving, and returning is the same love that Christ showed us, and it is the same love that we are called to show each other that reflects the deep structure of God. We could assert unequivocally that it is the love that leads to life—life eternal—the life of God.

LIFE

I came that they may have life, and have it abundantly.
(John 10:10)

I am the way, and the truth, and the life; no one comes
to the Father, but by me. (John 14:6)

We are not suggesting that the Christian community of faith is a nice add-on to our lives that makes them better. We are asserting unequivocally that the Christian community of faith is the very essence of life itself. We might even go so far as to suggest that without it we are the walking dead. We think we are alive. We wake up in the morning, eat breakfast, kiss the wife or husband and kids, drive to work, have meetings, discuss problems and opportunities, drive home, have dinner, kiss the kids goodnight, and repeat the process until we retire or kick the bucket. Is this all there is? We have other activities on weekends and vacations, but do these constitute the best life has to offer? Is there a grandeur that life can offer that is only accessible through life in Christ within a community of faith? In fact, what we call eternal life—the life of God—is precisely that new level of life, which has been made available to us through Christ *in community.*

The way the community of faith functions to develop all these and many more characteristics may be a bit of a mystery as the Holy Spirit is allowed to operate, but we can see some relationships that should give us some encouragement. We have an opportunity to express and experience *patience* at every turn as each member offers his or her thoughts in dialogue. We develop a deeper sense of *purity* and *chastity* when we recognize how self-centeredness destroys the very fabric of our relationships. We start to understand the power of *compassion* as we see how it allows members of our community to grow and flourish. We experience *joy* and *suffering* as we engage each other in *love* and *compassion*. Each of these virtues informs the others, and we access them by sharing our lives together with *honesty* and *trust*. In other words, the community of faith is the place where we learn to be more and more like Jesus and to live into the eternal life of God that has been offered to us.

While the feel of the community of faith has much to do with the transformation of individuals within the context of relationships, the light that shines forth has everything to do with the way these relationships look to those on the outside. Certainly it is true and important that each of us as individuals grow in love, patience, wisdom, knowledge, compassion, and so forth, but the real flowering of the community is the way it lights up the world around it, and offers it life—and life abundantly. This flowing outward—this glory of God—that attracts others into that light and life is the ultimate goal of our lives in Christ. Indeed, it is the "finish" of the community of faith that gives it the capacity to change the world.

18

THE "FINISH" OF CHRISTIAN COMMUNITY

Just as the "finish" of a car is the exterior look—the clarity and brilliance of the paint, the smoothness to the touch, the lines and symmetry, and the overall harmony of form and function—the "finish" of the community of faith is directly related to the vision of Christ's presence that is seen and experienced by the members and by outside observers. When others stop and look, they see the face of Christ in all the members, and they are washed by the love that is overflowing. You might say that the "finish" of the Christian community of faith is like a fountain whose drain is stopped up and is overflowing all over the street and grass and driveway and sidewalks and parking lots and on the floors of all the buildings in sight. It is moving outward like a flood engulfing everything in sight with the love of Christ.

We can also use the term "finish" in a different way to mean the goal or "finish line." The "finish" or goal, the achievement of which gives us our "finish" or luster, is none other than the transformation into the perfect likeness of Jesus Christ. Our goal is to reflect the glory of God by being perfect instruments of his will—just as Jesus was the perfect instrument of his Father's will.

Whether it can be done may depend on whether the initial parts can be made to "fit"—whether members of a parish or congregation are willing to allow God to *make* them "fit." Again, Pope Benedict offers some potent words:

> To live by faith and die for faith is possible only because the power of the living community, which it created and still creates, opens up the significance of history and renders it unequivocal in a way that no amount of mere reasoning could do.[65]

Here the "power of the living community" takes center stage as in many of his writings. What we would be asserting here is that the challenge before us as Christians is to develop a high understanding of what this "living community" could and should look like—and begin to build it wherever Christians gather. As long as we keep our communities shallow, programmatic, and incidental, we will continue to fail the call to unity and love that Jesus Christ announces in our hearts every moment of every day. We may not be able to induce the glory of God, but we certainly can see it flourish as Christians gather to experience and to express the Eleventh Commandment.

While the characteristics of an authentic Christian community of faith—what we have called its "feel"—can be seen

65 Joseph Ratzinger, *Church, Ecumenism, and Politics: New Endeavors in Ecclesiology* (San Francisco: Ignatius Press, 2008), 86–7.

as fruits of the community in and of themselves, we might take the opportunity to step back and look at some larger themes. Our growth as individuals takes place in relationship. Healthy relationships bring a life-giving environment, and a life-giving environment offers the world a hope for the future. While we have talked about the fruits of the Spirit yielding the "feel" or characteristics of a community of faith, here we direct our attention to aspects of healthy communities that are fruitful not only to individuals, but also to the larger society. Here are a few fruits that can spin off from the development and life of meaningful Christian communities of faith.

If the "finish" of the community of faith is the light and glory of God that shines forth and transforms the world, we then are driven to examine how that world could be changed as authentic Christian community springs up and flourishes. This outward looking energy begins with the process of evangelization.

EVANGELIZATION

Let your light so shine before men, that they may see your good works and give glory to your Father who is in heaven. (Matt 5:16)

Light and *glory*—the light that shines forth from the Christian community of faith *is* the glory of God on earth. People don't really see the glory of God in great cathedrals, in elaborate liturgies, or in profuse vestments, candles, and incense. All this may be a reflection of something deeper, but it is not the thing itself. The light and glory can only be shown in the love of Christ developed in and exhibited by the Christian community of faith. If we are indeed able to find or help create an authentic Christian community of faith and if it engenders the kind of joy, love, transparency, and life-giving experience that should arise, then we should want others to have the same experience. This is not intended to be a club within a club, but simply the expression that the apostles intended when they began to draw people into the life of Christ—this life that is now called Christianity. The vision of a Christian community of faith is realized when a stranger enters and he or she encounters the light of Christ in each of the people of God who are present. What could be more inviting than to see the love of Christ being acted out all around and experience the love of Christ from others? Until we can do this, I fear that Jesus might well say, "I never knew you." If we do not show this love, then we have no basis for calling ourselves his disciples. This may seem a bit harsh, but it may be just as harsh as the call to evangelize is compelling.

We can take our lead from two examples of evangelism in the Gospel of John:

> The next day again John was standing with two of his disciples; and he looked at Jesus as he walked, and said, "Behold the lamb of God!" . . . One of the two who heard John speak and followed him was Andrew, Simon Peter's brother. He first found his brother Simon and said to him, "we have found the Messiah." He brought Simon to Jesus . . . (John 1:35–40)

> Then the woman left her water-jar and went back to the city. She said to the people, "Come and see a man who told me everything I have

ever done! He cannot be the Messiah, can he?"
They left the city and were on their way to him.
(John 4:28)

Come and see! In both of these instances, people were so
moved by an experience of Jesus that they could not keep
from telling the "good news" to whomever would listen.
When we have such an experience in our own communities
of faith, an experience of the Christ in each other, we too
will not be able to hold it in and will want to share it with
others. The call to "Come and see!" should be both compelling and founded on a real delight in the expression of the
love of Christ in the community of faith.

Another powerful quotation comes from the prophet
Jeremiah:

> If I say, "I will not mention him, or speak any
> more in his name," there is in my heart as it were
> a burning fire shut up in my bones, and I am
> weary with holding it in, and I cannot. (Jer 20:9)

And I cannot! If we have had the experience of Christ in
each other, we will not be able to hold it in. We will be
compelled to spread the Good News. But what *is* the Good
News. We have heard of it since we were old enough to understand our Christian journey, but we may be fuzzy about
just exactly what it means. The following is the classic source
text from the Gospel of Luke:

> And he came to Nazareth, where he had been
> brought up; and he went to the synagogue, as his
> custom was, on the sabbath day. And he stood

up to read; and there was given to him the book
of the prophet Isaiah. He opened the book and
found the place where it was written, "The Spirit
of the Lord is upon me, because he has anoint-
ed me to preach good news to the poor. He has
sent me to proclaim release to the captives and
recovering of sight to the blind, to set at liberty
those who are oppressed, to proclaim the accept-
able year of the Lord." And he closed the book,
and gave it back to the attendant, and sat down;
and the eyes of all in the synagogue were fixed
on him. And he began to say to them, "Today
this scripture has been fulfilled in your hearing."
(Luke 4:16–21)

The Good News can, therefore, mean two things: (1) the
captives are freed, the blind see, and the poor are made rich
and (2) the very Incarnation of God, Jesus Christ, through
which the eternal life of God is made available to all of mankind, has arrived. In fact, as we now understand, freedom,
sight, and wealth are now interpreted in terms of the life of
Christ. There is no true freedom, sight, or wealth independent of a life in Christ. If we ourselves experience that release from the prison of sin, from the blindness to the truth
and from the poverty of soul, we can only wish to share that
Good News with others.

Again we must start at home. We really have nothing to
offer until we have a community of faith within our own
parish community. We can go to worship services every day,
but until we have put faith into practice in building an authentic community of faith, it has no real meaning. The first
step is to draw members of our own parish or congregation

into communion. You might find that to be a considerable challenge, depending on the culture from which you are starting. It may mean the transformation of a Bible study Sunday school class into a deliberate broader-based communal experience. It may mean the creation of spaces in which people can meet before you can start the process of building. It may mean weeklong missions, workshops, or a series of sermons to start to change expectations and open up new possibilities. Whatever needs to be done must be started at home and a process initiated to draw folks who are already there into community.

We might be tempted to believe this kind of internal evangelization is an easy and straightforward process. We could find, however, that it is more challenging than it looks. Recall the phenomenal success of Paul when evangelizing the Gentiles relative to the more modest success of Peter and James evangelizing those within the Jewish community. In a sense, we are more like Peter and James as we try to draw enthusiastic participants from a culture that has functioned for many years without what we are offering. Complacency and resistance to change are always more daunting challenges among those who may be satisfied with the fare that they are used to and with which they are comfortable. They have no idea what has been missing, let alone that they might need it.

Once we learn the joy of bringing other Christians to an authentic experience of the fullness of community in Christ, the logical thing to do is to reach out to those outside the Church. Many would say that we should concentrate on the un-churched, but there are many of other faiths who have never experienced people trying to be Christ to each other. As a matter of fact, we might stick our necks out here and gingerly suggest that the majority of Christians have never experienced this phenomenon—and an earth-shaking, life-altering phenomenon it would be. So if our Christian community of faith is indeed such a place, it should be the most attractive place on earth, and we should want to share it with everyone we meet. We should not only have the desire, but also a sense of obligation to draw folks into the Christian community of faith. Love and truth when married together are so irresistible that there should be few who cannot be attracted by their pull.

The process of looking outward has an important effect on the way individual virtues are completed. We could say that the "finish" of individual virtues that we have called the "feel" of the community of faith is only completed as those virtues look outward. The result is an integration of all the parts of the human person—his or her body, mind, and spirit in accord with the will of God.

INDIVIDUAL INTEGRITY

The word *integrity* can be interpreted on a number of different levels. Politicians often talk about their *integrity*—meaning that they do not lie, cheat, or steal. The Watergate scandal might be seen as a breakdown of personal *integrity*. The dalliances of Jim Baker may be another.[66] On a bit higher plane, the word might refer to one who is *integrated*. All of the various parts that make up our person—our physical, mental, and spiritual characteristics—are in harmony. In other words, we are consistent. The highest level of integrity, however, would refer to the idea that not only are we internally consistent, but we are also operating in accord with who we were intended to be. An automobile or computer that functions

66 Jim Baker was a televangelist in the 1980s who was caught up in a sexual liaison with a co-worker.

as it was intended to function would have this sort of integrity. In the case of human beings, if we are to talk of this kind of integrity, we must assume a creator God that made us with something "in mind." For some this might be more of a stretch, but for Christians this is a fundamental assumption of life. We believe that each of us as individuals has God-given talents and characteristics that make us unique and priceless. As the psalmist said:

> I praise you because I am fearfully and wonderfully made; your works are wonderful, I know that full well. (Ps 139:14 NIV)

As creatures of God, we inspire awe and wonder. We have each been formed with some larger purpose in mind than merely to be born, live a subsistence life, and die—like a cricket or an amoeba. We were made in the image of God, which means that we have precious characteristics of God built into us. What this implies is a level of integrity that relates specifically to our creation by God. This level of integrity means that we are to function as God intended for us to function—we would call that the will of God. This might be quite a dilemma were it not for Jesus Christ. We Christians believe that Jesus showed us who we are intended to be as human beings. In other words, the premiere human being, the one who represents perfect *integrity*, is none other than Jesus Christ himself. Because each part of his being functioned in perfect accord with every other part, and all parts functioned in perfect accord with the will of the Father, Jesus becomes our benchmark model of integrity—integrity at its highest level.

If the ultimate goal of the community of faith is the

transformation of individuals into the perfect likeness of Jesus Christ; and for Christians, Jesus represents the highest form of integrity; then the development of individual integrity becomes one of the implied goals of the Christian community of faith. As a life of love is developed, the pieces of our individual puzzles should start to come together. Our hopes and dreams start to line up with our capacities and capabilities. As our transparency increases, our ability to see ourselves as God sees us also increases. As a result, we have the opportunity to live into the truth rather than live out of our own delusions. As sin is driven off, that which keeps us from the love and truth of God is diminished and our access to the eternal life offered to us by Jesus Christ is increased. Thus, we become more and more *integrated*. All this at least has the potential of happening as an essential fruit of our lives in Christian community.

In this context it is worthwhile to talk about the relationship between integrity and *ordering*—giving order to all the aspects of our being. When we say that sin causes a disordering of our being, we are really talking about the way in which integrity is disrupted. If we say that an inclination toward sin is a disordered state, what we mean is that our integrity as a human being is disrupted. Often we use the word *disorder* to mean an illness—a breakdown of physiological integrity. In this kind of usage, the pieces of the biological puzzle are not functioning as they were intended. But what exactly do we mean by order and disorder *in our being*? This is a bit trickier, because our reference point for order in being cannot be gauged with biological measurements such as white blood cell counts, estrogen levels, or amounts of cholesterol in the blood. In fact, even psychology has difficulty defining subtly disordered states. In general, psychologists and psychiatrists are more concerned with functionality than optimality. They really do not have any way to discern or define what is optimal. Christians, on the other hand, have a model of optimality—Jesus Christ. The challenge is to explore how he was *ordered*. Now, this is where it gets interesting. What are the parts of the puzzle we are most concerned to order and what do we mean by ordering them? Here we might be stepping out on a bit of a limb. This may be some new territory. And while elucidating the details of this terrain may be far beyond the scope of this discussion, we might point toward some helpful concepts.

Imagine being placed in a number of situations in which you must respond. The way in which you respond is directly related to your ordering. For example, someone says to you that you have bad breath. What is the first thought that pops into your head? "How dare you!" or "Oh no, I must be a bad person," or "Really, do you have a mint?" Each of these responses has to do with the ordering of our being. Do we look at truth as always a good in itself, or do we evaluate everything in terms of ourselves? Do we start with compassion or love and work our way down to defense and security, or do we do it the other way around? As we look at Jesus as our model, we constantly ask these kinds of questions. What were the central organizing principles of his very being? If we say that his central organizing principle was love, then we need to understand what kind of love he was offering and how it *ordered* his life accordingly.

We can see that this ordering process may be just as complex as the biological ordering processes that allow our human bodies to function. The community of faith is therefore like a hospital for helping us help each other to place the pieces of our being *in order*—to eliminate the "disorders" of our being. As we engage one another with this in mind, we would expect to see a gradual reordering to the way Jesus was ordered and a consequent growth in integrity as the pieces are ordered as they were intended to be. This integrity, that itself was a product of entering into relationships in the community of faith and a process of that community's looking outward, influences the way in which all other relationships are formed.

HEALTHY FRIENDSHIPS

Friendships can take on a wide range of forms. There are friendships based on like interests such as stamp collecting (as C. S. Lewis loved to point out) or a love of NASCAR racing. These kinds of friendships flourish in the context in which they are originally formed, but may not grow beyond those boundaries. There are deeper friendships that can form as a result of common sets of values such as might be formed in the Young Democrats Club or the Young Republicans Club. Friendships can also form within community service organizations like Kiwanis, Lions, or Sertoma. While all of these kinds of friendships are based on some form of commonality, the most important commonality, at least from a Christian point of view, is the common faith in the saving life of Jesus Christ. In its highest form, such a friendship should be called a *spiritual friendship*.

Spiritual friendships are not common, even within the community of faith, but when they do occur, they have a strong resemblance to the kinds of relationships that Jesus entered into and encouraged.

> No longer do I call you servants, for the servant does not know what his master is doing; but I

have called you friends, for all that I have heard
from my Father I have made known to you.
(John 15:15)

This kind of friendship is based on a shared journey toward the eternal life that has been offered to us through
Christ. It is rich, transparent, full of joy, secure, and life-giving. While we might not expect to form this kind of friendship in all of our relationships in the community of faith, the
possibility should be present and even likely. As we grow in
our lives in Christ, we should grow in our ability to form
these kinds of friends—friends to whom we relate as Jesus
modeled and taught. In this way, we certainly would be a
gift to them and they to us in the same way that Jesus Christ
is a *gift* to us all. These kinds of friendships do not necessarily presuppose any religious requirements. Integrity, honesty, patience, and love can function independently of worship and sacraments. The point here is that *all* friendships are
made healthier with the basic virtues that can be learned and
practiced in an authentic community of faith. Solid friendships should add not only meaning to our own lives, but also
add depth and meaning to all those with whom we come in
contact. The most important relationships in which healthy
friendships are crucial are those consummated in marriage.

FULFILLING MARRIAGE AND HEALTHY FAMILIES

One of our greatest challenges in an age of self-interest is to
understand the highest possibilities in marriage and how to
bring that about. In fact, a Christian marriage is a little community of faith. We sometimes use metaphors from marriage
to inform our understanding of a healthy community, but in
reality the reverse might be more valuable. Because we do

not choose the members of our community of faith as we do our spouse, the challenge is considerably greater to learn how to love as Christ loved in a community of faith that we did not choose.[67] All of the characteristics of an authentic community of faith apply even more so to the community of Christian marriage. One would hope that as these characteristics are modeled and developed in a healthy community of faith, married couples who participate in the community are brought to a keener understanding of how these same characteristics should be operative in their married lives. Too often marriage is seen as an accommodation rather than a celebration of differences. We fail to learn how to engage each other in meaningful dialogue such that we learn who our spouse is at his or her deepest level. We consequently fail to share our true selves with each other. The more we posture the more we grow apart until the bond breaks or both spouses retreat into a kind of safe isolation.

All too often a couple will be unable to be transparent because there are areas of their being that they are protecting. It is only when we can be truly "naked" psychologically and spiritually with each other that transparency and deep connection become a possibility. As we begin to be transparent with one another, we attain the possibility of becoming our true selves and of sharing that with our spouse as well as with our children. The fact is, we really cannot hide in our family—we just think we can. We think we are fooling the rest of the members of our family, but unless they are blind or so self-absorbed that they care

---

67 This discussion is so very loaded, coming from one who has never been married. I have been informed that often we don't even marry the person we thought we were marrying, and that the community of faith and a marriage might in many cases be much more similar than I am suggesting.

nothing for anyone else, they know who we are. We just don't want to accept that they know—and that barrier to *shared* knowledge is what keeps us from being in true communion with the other members of our family.

It should be noted that the inherent intimacy of a marriage and family offers wondrous opportunities and demands for developing true community. It may be only through judicious efforts that we resist those opportunities and demands and somehow insist on unhealthy relationships. As the community of faith develops the kinds of healthy loving relationships that are in accord with our lives in Christ, so should it help develop the kinds of healthy, loving relationships that make our families full of steadfast life, joy, and hope. As families grow in healthy loving relationships, so should they help develop the kinds of healthy, loving relationships that make the community of faith full of steadfast life, joy, and hope. We might, therefore, suggest that the mutual struggles for intimacy and community, both within our parishes and within the families that make up those parishes, can yield wondrous possibilities for sharing and growing together.

TRANSFORMING PARISHES AND CONGREGATIONS

It would be wonderful if we simply could equate the congregation with the community of faith, but, as we mentioned, parishes are often much too large to function in this way. Even smaller parishes are not clear on how intentionally to function as a true community of faith. Renewal movements have repeatedly tried to reinvigorate the communal life of the parish with little or only fleeting success. Traveling evangelists are brought in, and annual intensive weeklong "missions" with outside speakers and additional worship services

are instituted in order to breathe new life into church congregations. Ultimately, however, unless there is an authentic
community of faith, no amount of renewal or reinvigoration
will help. The apostolic model of twelve and Jesus Christ is
still worth intentionally emulating. The emphasis here is on
intentionality. As we have said, parishes can be overwhelmed
with programs and ministries that absorb great amounts of
time and resources without forming the seedbed for true
community. Ministries likewise may have the look and feel
of endeavors that reflect the love of Christ, often without
getting below the surface of a communal life in Christ. These
ministries are nominally Christian, but the participants never
see the depth of possibilities that Christ intended for us. In
our relationships with one another, serving together can and
should be the basis for expressing, if not necessarily building,
community. We just need to use care in how we execute
ministries so that they are a reflection of the love of Christ,
not only toward those being ministered to, but also among
those who are ministering.

The challenge in any effort to develop true community
is to start small and grow to the point where everyone in
the parish is at first offered an opportunity to participate and
eventually is exposed to the fruits of a true community of
faith. If this can happen, the life of the parish can be renewed
and reinvigorated from within in such a way that a perma-
nent transformation takes place—a transformation that is re-
sistant to crisis and immune to failures in parish leadership.

If this transformation is done well, the parish can exhibit
a level of continuity that can actually be a place of learning
for new clergy. I have been a member of a church that was
known as a teaching church. Such churches are also known
as "clergy makers." Their maturity surpasses the maturity of

new clergy that pass through their doors. Pastors learn how to be pastors in churches like this. The University Baptist and Brethren Church was one of these. On the other hand, some churches are known as "clergy eaters." They devour clergy because the leaders of the congregation are consumed by ravenous self-interest. A true community of faith will not allow that kind of unhealthy behavior to survive. To the benefit of all, this kind of behavior will not withstand the heat of the refiner's fire—the love of Christ as exhibited in an authentic community of faith. While the community can positively influence unhealthy parishioners, the same thing could be said about unhealthy clergy—they will not survive the refiner's fire without being transformed. Clergy need desperately to be *participants* in a community of faith. Often the degree to which they are isolated is precisely the degree to which they can maintain unhealthy lives that ultimately will adversely affect or destroy the congregation entrusted to their care. If you have an authentic community of faith, fan the flame. If you don't have one, start to form one as soon as possible. The health, the soul, and possibly the very existence of your parish may be at stake.

As we start to see our parishes as a microcosm of the larger society, we begin to see them also as a model for the society as a whole.

HEALTHY SOCIETIES

Societies have many of the same characteristics as communities of faith. They are communities that rely on relationships to function. If the relationships are healthy—they are open, honest, and caring—the society will be healthy. Small rural communities often function in this way, because there is a perceived interdependence that demands these kinds of relationships for survival. This was especially true of the small farm communities that preceded the industrial revolution. Everyone knew each other. Children were born to the shared joy of the community, they went to school together, played together, grew up together, and often married each other—to start the cycle of life all over again. Families shared resources, especially "man-power." Members of the community worshiped together, celebrated together, marched off to war together, and mourned their losses together. There was little sense of isolation or alienation. For good or ill, everyone knew what everyone else was up to. There was little place to hide—both physically and psychologically. With the coming of the industrial revolution, mobility increased manifold. Young adults left town for greater opportunities. Others came to town to fill the gaps, and the possibility of anonymity grew. The progression of this trend has continued until we arrive at our "modern" society.

I live in Denver, Colorado—the home of the Columbine High School shooting (April 20, 1999) and the Aurora Theater shooting (July 20, 2012). As a result of these two horrific events, people are understandably trying to do *something* in response: get rid of the guns, improve the state and federal mental health programs, or place armed guards everywhere. Let me propose that none of these purported solutions have anything whatsoever to do with the real problem facing our modern society. The real problem is one of community. Robert Nisbet in his seminal work, *The Quest for Community,* talks at length of the breakdown of the church, family, and town communities.[68] Probably the most dramatic influences on communal life have been the roles of technology, large

68 Robert Nisbet, *The Quest for Community* (Wilmington, DE: ISI Books, 1990), 39–89.

corporations, and the state. As technology allows for and encourages specialization and individualization, we share less and less in common. I don't need to go to a concert when I can plug my mp3 player into my ears and jog to the specific tunes I have downloaded for my own personal enjoyment—to the exclusion of all those around me. I drive my car with tinted windows so others are excluded from my world—I can't wave hello, because they can't see me. I don't travel in wagon trains that required intense cooperation—I pack into a jumbo jet, face the back of the seat ahead of me, plug in my headset and simply achieve my one narrow goal of reaching my destination with only minor engagement of those around me. I drive my own car, because car-pooling does not offer me the personal flexibility I desire. I press the remote garage-door opener and disappear into the confines of my home, without seeing or interacting with anyone. When I venture out, I can reverse the process, avoiding all social contact with my neighbors if I so choose.[69] If I live in a condo or apartment, I don't even see neighbors when I am mowing the lawn, because I don't have a lawn to mow. It is all very efficient—but isolating.

Large corporations have impacted communal life in a number of ways. I shop at huge stores that give vast variety of products without knowing or wanting to know the other shoppers or the employees of the store. I am self-reliant, self-contained, and isolated—efficient, but isolated. Work in large corporations also takes on a different communal aspect. Specialization results in my interacting with one supervisor, a few co-workers, and in certain cases those to whom I may provide services. I may interact superficially at the company picnic, but seldom develop intimate relationships as I might

---

69 My friend, Ted Straughan, gave me this insight.

in a small company struggling for survival. We might go so far as to suggest that as efficiency and individualization increases through technology and economies of scale, community decreases. In other words, community is messy and inefficient. Unfortunately, it may also be the essence of life.

More and more, municipal, state, and federal governments supply goods and services that displace those that used to be provided through communal enterprise. Water and electric power come from municipalities or state-contracted utilities. Mail is delivered through the US Postal Service. Welfare is provided by state and federal agencies. A "single payer" healthcare system is gradually displacing individual payers with individual responsibility. Insurance companies have an increasing influence on how healthcare is provided in an increasingly "efficient" system—a system in which we are gradually losing the intimacy of the family doctor who used to be practically another member of the family.

This discussion is not in any way intended to be a diatribe against modern trends or a polemic for or against any political agenda. It is simply a call to more deliberate forms of community. If we do not get community in ways that were common in more primitive societies, we need to construct, support, and participate in forms of community that replace older forms. The community of faith, therefore, is not a nice addition to our Christian lives, but might just be the glue that holds the social fabric of our lives together. This fabric is what gives meaning and stability to individual lives. When this fabric falls apart, even if, or especially if it happens silently and stealthily over decades, isolation and alienation are the inevitable result. What we are seeing in the shootings and bombings all around the world may be the direct effect of a breakdown of the social fabric that used to force all of us to work together for the sake of survival. The history of these relationships has been anything but stellar. Hatred has at times been rampant and recalcitrant, but underlying all this error has been an understanding, at least by some, that we do depend on one another. The idea that someone would simply kill a bunch of people and then kill himself was inconceivable. The perpetrators seem to exist in a state of isolation and alienation. The impersonal term "perpetrators" even implies a sense of separation and alienation. It is not my cousin or brother or neighbor, but the *perpetrator* whom I don't know and really don't care to know. Let's just pack this unknown entity off to prison and be rid of the problem. Only "the problem" keeps rearing its ugly head like Medusa or Whack-a-Mole. And we have built this isolating and alienating society ourselves, so it is up to us to fix it. We have to start from scratch to build some communities that are worthy of the name. This means that we Christians must start where we live, in our parishes and congregations, and begin to rebuild the fabric of life—life in relationship—life in the community of faith. This place where we live—where we dwell—becomes our vineyard in which we toil for the good of all. It is this broadest of all perspectives that drives our desire for unity among all humanity—both Christian and non-Christian alike.

AUTHENTIC ECUMENISM

Ecce quam bonum habitare fratres in unum. This happens to be the motto of my undergraduate college, The University of the South at Sewanee, Tennessee. It means "Behold, how good and pleasant it is when brothers dwell in unity!" and comes from Psalm 133. This call to unity among Christian brethren resounds in the hearts of all who lament the great divisions that exist in the Body of Christ. As a Catholic, I can point toward a compelling statement in the *Catechism of the Catholic Church* concerning ecumenism or Christian unity.

> From the beginning, this one Church has been marked by a great *diversity* which comes from both the variety of God's gifts and the diversity of those who receive them. Within the unity of the People of God, a multiplicity of peoples and cultures is gathered together. Among the Church's members, there are different gifts, offices, conditions, and ways of life. "Holding a rightful place in the communion of the Church there are also particular Churches that retain their own traditions." The Great richness of such diversity is not opposed to the Church's unity. Yet sin and the burden of its consequences constantly threaten the gift of unity. And so the Apostle has to exhort Christians to "maintain the unity of the Spirit in the bond of peace (Eph 4:3)."[70]

The documents of Vatican II also speak directly to this unity:

> . . . what does most to show God's presence clearly is the brotherly love of the faithful who, being all of one mind and spirit, work together for the faith of the gospel and present themselves as a sign of unity.[71]

---

70 *Catechism of the Catholic Church* (Vatican: Libreria Editrice Vaticana, 1997), paragraph 814.
71 Gaudium et Spes, *Vatican Council II, The Conciliar and Postconciliar*

Through my experiences in many different denominations, I have found that there is one common denominator that connects all Christians—the yearning for a community of faith that reflects the love of Christ. No one seems to argue about the meaning of the Eleventh Commandment. We might all have different opinions about what that love entails, but that would be true *within* denominations, as much as it might be true *between* denominations. The community of faith says little explicitly about doctrine, polity, or church culture. This love of Christ seems to be the one unifying aspect of our faith and yet the one we may need the most work on.

Some have said that our unity is in our belief in Jesus Christ, but that clearly has a lot to do with doctrine, specifically the branch of doctrine called Christology. Some have said that our unity arises in our service to others, but service can be offered by believers and non-believers alike, and as we have said, service by itself can also be a distraction from the development of true community. Others see our unity in our willingness to share an ecumenical worship service. Some just want to "weave."[72] Thus, our understanding of unity often simply comes from our desire to express that unity in some outward form. In other words, we may have a rather romantic notion of Christian unity, but when the rubber hits the road, we find our differences keep us from any meaningful shared understanding of who we are as Christians and where we are going—together.

This division need not always be the case, however. One powerful example of true ecumenical ministry is Kairos

---

Documents, (Northport, New York: Costello Publishing Company, 2004), 921.
72 This reference comes from the song, "Weave, weave, weave us together, weave us together in unity and love," by Rosemary Crow, 1982.

Prison Ministry. It is an outgrowth of Cursillo, a short course in Christianity for those who desire a renewal in their faith.[73] Kairos, which means "God's time," is made up of Protestant and Catholic men and women who minister to those in prison. The central activity is a four-day weekend in which "residents" hear and discuss talks given by team members as a basis for building a small embryonic community of faith. In fact the team-building effort that precedes each weekend is itself an intensive community-building exercise that exhibits many aspects of an authentic community of faith.

What is most interesting and compelling about Kairos from an ecumenical viewpoint is the requirement that denominational differences be avoided. The motto of the ministry is, "Listen, listen; love, love." In other words, the core understanding of this Christian ministry is the sharing of the love of Christ. While denominational differences often rear their heads, the consensus is always to move back toward the common foundation on which all team members rest— the sharing the love of Christ with those who may not have heard or felt it before.[74]

Any movement of Christians "together" in unity not only includes a gathering of individuals, but also a gathering of ecclesial bodies. Individuals can come together in joint ministries, such as Kairos, and ecumenical worship services, and these are of great value as recognition of our desire for unity. But the real challenge may be for the larger ecclesial bodies to start to recognize the depth of our connectedness as

---

73 More on this in the chapter entitled "The Current Context."

74 I joined my first Kairos team in February of 2014. At the time of this writing, I have not participated in my first weekend, but all who have shared their experiences with me assure me that not only are the residents changed but those on the team as well. People in Kairos keep participating in the ministry because of the profound effect it has had on their lives.

Christians and the true basis for a meaningful ecumenism.

So, where *are* we going? While any community of faith has as its underpinnings a set of beliefs or doctrinal assumptions, the results of those beliefs and how they are manifest in a community seem to appear very similar. If they are *not* similar, it may be that we have become massively distracted by concepts and practices that have little to do with our transformation into the perfect likeness of Jesus Christ, who is love personified. The common language of experience, dialogue, prayer, play, etc. should level the playing field. To some degree we all recognize what love feels like in community, even though we might not know how we got it, let alone how to get it. At a deeper level, however, we inevitably get to the place where we are confronted with the ultimate possibility of transformation—the transformation of a group into a loving community of faith and the transformation of individuals within that group into looking more and more like Jesus. As Christians, this transformation has everything to do with our understanding of Jesus Christ: who he was, what he accomplished and what he passed on to us. I would contend that when the community starts to bump up against its need to articulate and refine its understanding of Jesus Christ, it already has made huge strides in being "one" in love. As the community becomes more and more deliberate in its self-understanding, the greater potential it has to grow into an authentic transformative Christian community of faith.

This fact might be the reason why interdenominational ministries like Renovaré[75] seem to work so well with a wide variety of Protestant denominations represented and even a few Catholics (like me). The more that Christians come

---

75 More on this in the chapter entitled "The Current Context."

together with a common interest in a specific topic, the
more we find that the underlying desire to reflect the love
of Christ forms the real common bond of unity that we all
experience as Christians. There is no question that we have
different ways of worshipping and different ways of expressing what we believe. As Cynthia de Berry Freeman would
say, "Sometimes we prays before we sings, and sometimes we
sings before we prays."[76] On the other hand, we should find
that all of our doctrines and practices are, in fact, grounded
in our process of transformation. They are there as an integrated whole that always points toward that transformation.
If, however, we allow these doctrines and practices to swamp
our transformation in community, we simply have missed the
point.

One of the most challenging pieces of Scripture is the
following:

> Go therefore and make disciples of all nations,
> baptizing them in the name of the Father and of
> the Son and of the Holy Spirit, teaching them
> to observe all that I have commanded you; and
> lo, I am with you always, to the close of the age.
> (Matt 28:19–20)

Here Jesus is assuming a unity centered on himself and the
act of baptism as a sign of that unity. He did not say go out
and make up a bunch of different rituals according to your
own desires and make up a bunch of different ideas vaguely
based on what I have said. Clearly, the assumption was that
what he had established with the apostles was solid enough
for them to draw folks into what we understand as the Body

76 Personal communication in a sermon.

of Christ—the living Church on earth that would survive
and flourish after he was gone. In fact, therein lies both the
rub and the possibility. As Jesus said:

> Nevertheless I tell you the truth: it is to your ad-
> vantage that I go away, for if I do not go away,
> the Counselor will not come to you; but if I go, I
> will send him to you. (John 16:7)

If he had stayed he might have been able to control the
spread of his Gospel, but we would have, in a sense, been
"tied to his apron strings." We would have been spiritually
crippled. It is only through our own willingness to be led
by the Holy Spirit that we can attain to the possibility of
sons and daughters of God. But unfortunately, we must tread
many diverse and sinful paths before we find our way back
to God. Adam and Eve started the wandering, Jesus offered
us the way back, but ultimately we must take responsibility
for our own journey, both as individuals and as communities. Just as the opportunity for an individual to find God
is always calling, the opportunity for the diverse and often
contradictory expressions of the Christian faith to find God
in community is always screaming louder.

In his book, *Church, Ecumenism, and Politics: New Endeavors in Ecclesiology*, a compilation of writings from the early to
mid-1980s, Pope Benedict discusses some foundational concepts of Church as the People of God and the hope for any
ecumenical progress to be based on a consensus regarding
the nature of authority, the definition of tradition, and finally, the reality of the Eucharist. In so doing, he repeatedly
refers to the fundamental nature of the life of the community of faith, whether that community exists within the larger

Christian body, among the leadership, or within individual congregations or parishes. In it, Pope Benedict observes:

> [The discussion of a synod of Catholic bishops] ought to be the effort of communal listening to the conscience of faith and thus help the members to understand the faith better with one another, so that they might also give better witness to it, based on such a communal understanding. . . . It is not a question of producing something new; rather, in freeing ourselves from what is merely personal, which separates us from one another, we are to discover the common answer of faith . . . [77]

While he is talking about Catholic bishops here, the same kind of communal intercourse is operative in any community of faith, especially one that is composed of members of different Christian denominations. If we are indeed created in the same image of God, and if we all believe in that image, we can start to trust the dialogue as it reflects that image in each of us. The community of faith is a place—maybe the only place—where this kind of deep meaningful dialogue can take place.

The rather recent realization that God is probably not pleased with us Christians because of our lack of unity, has set us on a path of *ecumenism*—the idea that the various Christian denominations should—no, *must*—try to get back together. It is not that diversity is bad. The Church has always had wondrous diversity, which served as the engine of our search for truth, love, and God. Unfortunately we see

77 Ratzinger, *Church, Ecumenism, and Politics*, 63.

ourselves as separate because of our differences of opinion regarding the importance of liturgy, the primacy of sacraments, the structure of our leadership, the importance of the historical lineage of Church and traditions, and the decorations in our worship spaces. The primary issue, however, is centered on the underlying differences of opinion regarding the person of Jesus Christ and the nature of God. These in turn influence the way in which we live out our understandings of love and truth. It is these more profound differences that keep us from enjoying true unity in Christ.

And yet many Christians yearn for unity. As we said, our dialogue often centers on innocuous statements like, "Well, we all believe in Jesus" or "We can come together in service to the poor" or we could just decide to put our arms around each other and "weave." They are all lovely notions, but as far as bringing the diverse denominations together, they may be just wishful thinking. What we do have in common, however, is an appreciation of the need for community. I have never found a Christian church that did not yearn for more community. This universal yearning may be the one common denominator among all Christians. We are not just talking about "chips and dip and fellowship," but the deep kind of community whose sole purpose is to grow and reflect the love of Christ. If we could agree on that kind of community as a common goal, then we could start to engage each other on unifying questions: What is love? Who is God? Who is Christ? And who am I? When we can start to explore answers to these questions, ones which directly relate to the way in which we form community, we will see that we are all in the same boat and there is only one direction in which that boat can move—toward fullness in the love of Jesus Christ—toward a full and joyful acting out of the

Eleventh Commandment.

Once we have a compelling desire to form and be a participant in an authentic Christian community of faith, we are immediately challenged to *do it*. It is easy to read and nod our heads in agreement (assuming that at least one or two readers will do this), but it is an entirely different matter actually to pull it off. Throughout the history of the Church, there have been daunting challenges to the creation of a Christian community of faith. These challenges persist and are even more daunting today. What are these challenges that form the context in which we must work, if we are to pursue our desire for legitimate Christian community? The next part will try to address some of these challenges and offer an example of one effort to surmount them.

PART IV

CHALLENGES

19

AN HISTORICAL PERSPECTIVE

The early Church, as reflected in the Acts of the Apostles, was established as a series of communities that worshiped together, lived together, shared possessions in common, and saw their journey toward fullness in Christ not only as an individual one, but also as a communal one. Most of the letters of Paul preserved in Holy Scripture are letters to communities of faith (the exceptions being those to Timothy, Titus, and Philemon). He saw each community as a whole, and they must have consequently seen themselves as a whole, moving organically toward the goal of Christ Jesus. The only thing we know about these early communities is what we see in the Acts of the Apostles. They were relatively small—on the order of hundreds rather than thousands of members. They were forced into a high level of cohesiveness because of the periodic persecution that they experienced.[78] They shared

---

78 There seems to be a debate going on as to whether the early Christians were indeed persecuted or just punished for failing to fall in line with what were then simply "legal" requirements, such as requiring everyone in the empire to make a sacrifice to the emperor's divine spirit or forcing people

their wealth and belongings in a way that would be consistent with our modern understanding of a commune. Clearly, there is no mention of multiple services or other kinds of divisions. The Corinthian, Colossian, Ephesian, Philippian, Thessalonian, Galatian, Roman, and Jerusalem communities probably functioned similarly. Their unity was inherent to their size, their common external pressures, and their common faith as presented in the letters of Paul.

As we move out of the apostolic period into the formation of the formal Church structure, a hierarchy centered on the chair of St. Peter implies that the Church sought to preserve that sense of unity—a unity that was later enhanced by the presence of bishops, a common statement of faith, a common worship centered on a shared meal remembering the death, resurrection, and ascension of Jesus, and ultimately a shared Scripture tradition. Early on, this Scripture tradition was simply a collection of writings passed around among the various communities, the letters of Paul being the earliest of such writings. One of the earliest listings of writings of the New Testament period was articulated by Irenaeus, Bishop of Lyon, in about AD 180, as an attempt to certify those writings that were orthodox and separate out those that were not. Subsequent councils of the Church adjusted and lent authority to the list that has been passed down as our New Testament "canon." During this period, creedal statements of faith

---

to partake of meat that had been sacrificed to idols. Candida Moss, a proponent of the idea that the persecution of early Christians was a "myth" (meaning a story that is not true), asserts that Christians were not generally sought out for their belief in such arcane concepts as the Trinity or the Incarnation, for example. Critics suggest that she is nit-picking, if Christian's fundamental beliefs caused them to refuse to obey laws and thereby become inherently dangerous to the perceived stability of the state. Most church historians clearly mark periods of persecution.

were developed that clarified aspects of the Christ event that were causing confusion among the faithful. As a part of the same ongoing process, liturgical forms were developed and standardized.

This process worked well until the issue of leadership surfaced. The first and possibly most profound change came with the conversion to Christianity of the Roman emperor, Constantine I. With the Edict of Milan in 313, Constantine proclaimed tolerance for all religions throughout the whole empire. In one stroke, the pressure that had, in a certain sense, formed the unity of the early Church was gone. As part of the process, the emperor became an important factor in the leadership of the Church. Unity of the Church became consonant with unity of the empire, and the emperor therefore had a strong stake in both. Councils were called and influenced by the state. The Christian leadership itself had a new stake in its relationship to the state, and controversies within the Church caused conflict within the empire.

From the conversion of Constantine until the 12th century, the Eastern Church was centered in Constantinople and the Western Church was centered in Rome. Rome was greatly influenced by the development of Roman law and therefore took on a form that tended to be more formal and legalistic. The Eastern Church was greatly influenced by its spiritual tradition which tended to focus on the mystical aspects of the faith.[79] From a leadership point of view, Rome argued that, as the original seat of St. Peter, it had primacy. Constantinople was unwilling to recognize that primacy, leading to the Great Schism in 1054, dividing the Roman Catholic Church,

---

79 This tradition could be said to have been greatly influenced by the Greek writings of authors centered in Antioch and Alexandria, such as Clement, Athanasius, Tertullian, and Origen.

centered in Rome, from the Eastern Orthodox Church, centered in Constantinople. The Roman Catholic branch of the Church trundled along for another four hundred years as the undisputed center of western Christendom until the Protestant Reformation in the 1500s. Martin Luther recognized a number of abuses being practiced under the auspices of the Roman Church, eventually posting his 95 Theses on the door of the Cathedral at Worms in 1517. Basically, as was the custom in academic circles, the theses were simply a call to debate. They were certainly not a call for a new church or a schism within the Catholic Church. The development and ramifications of the Protestant Reformation are indeed complex and far beyond the scope of this discussion. What we are looking for, however, is some indication of the impact the Reformation had on the structure of worship and communal life within the various denominations that evolved from the breakup of the western Church.

There are two major Protestant premises that influenced faith formation: the elevation of the idea of the priesthood of all believers and the primacy of Scripture alone. Although the original causes of the schism centered on clerical abuses, once the break was made, the floodgates were open for a wide range of changes, from the style of leadership to the nature of worship. The hierarchical and authoritative structure of the Catholic Church was seen as stifling the spiritual formation of believers. Consequently, individuals were elevated in their importance by doing away with the priesthood and by giving individuals responsibility for their own relationship to God and their own enlightenment by the Holy Spirit of the meaning of Scripture. It was clear that if the ultimate authority was going to be Scripture as interpreted by individuals, then individuals needed to be trained in the content of the Bible. Even though the early councils defined the Christian Bible, composed of both the Hebrew Bible—the Old Testament—and the New Testament, Protestantism took that canon as an enduring foundation upon which all faith was to be based. Once you have the Bible, you don't need a hierarchical structure to tell you what to believe, even though the Bible itself was a product of precisely that kind of hierarchical authoritative structure. This new emphasis on Scripture and individual responsibility had two profound and useful consequences—the *need* for the education of the common Christian in Scripture content and meaning as well as the development of a *mechanism* of informing the newly empowered priesthood of all believers. If they were to interpret Scripture based on their own engagement with the Holy Spirit, they needed to be empowered with knowledge of Scripture. One of the forms that this empowerment through education eventually took was adult Sunday school. It took the Catholic Church until Vatican II in the 1960s to articulate boldly the same principles of individual responsibility and the need for all believers to have accessibility to an understanding of Scripture.

While Sunday school had the basic intention of informing the masses, it had the added benefit of encouraging community through a more intimate engagement of parishioners in the process of learning and discussing not only scriptural *content*, but also, and possibly more importantly, scriptural *meaning*. As the Catholic Church was engaged in a two-thousand-year process of protecting the deposit of faith as delivered to the apostles, the Protestant churches were engaged in empowering individuals to develop their "personal relationship with Jesus." We might suggest that to some observers the former was more concerned with the *content* of the faith and the

latter was more concerned with the *activity* of the faith alone
(without any reference to obligatory actions). At the same
time, oddly enough, the Catholic Church seemed to some to
be stressing *works* (such as mass attendance and acts of pen-
ance), while the Protestant reformers were stressing *faith*. On
the surface it appears that the Catholics were being criticized
as believing in a "works-based righteousness" without any
reference to faith, and Protestants were being criticized for
believing in "righteousness by faith alone" without any responsibility for "works" of charity. As usual, this is a gross
simplification, but once these distinctions are articulated, it
should be just as evident that the content and the activity of
our faith must work together. The content of faith (*what* we
believe) without the activity of faith (*how* we believe) is just
an intellectual exercise. And the activity of faith without the
apostolic content results in a vast divergence from the intended goal of salvation history. Also, faith and works go hand in
hand—faith without works is dead, and works without faith
is simply social welfare or an empty tallying without transformation. In fact, both Catholics and Protestants would assert that they represent a proper balance of apostolic teaching,
faith, and works.

Here is another interesting comparison from one who has
observed from both sides of the Tiber. Catholics tend to deal
in "sins" and Protestants tend to deal in "sinfulness." The
former sees specific sins as acts of the will. The latter sees
sinfulness as a condition of our humanity. The breathtaking
conclusion is that both are true. There clearly are conscious
acts that we engage in, such as those enumerated in the Ten
Commandments,[80] which we know are wrong—and we do
them anyway. We should be prepared to ask for God's mercy

---

80 Or the Ten Words in the Jewish tradition.

and forgiveness in these instances. We might even be called to ask for the forgiveness of someone we have wronged. But to limit our concern only to those acts of will is to fail to address the fact that we all fall short of the glory of God. This too we must take responsibility for. We are all called to grow in our faith. Jesus grows us up and asks us to take responsibility for our own personal "falling short."

Because of these divergent perceptions, we might assert unequivocally that *we need each other*. We don't need just a little bit of each other or figuratively some of each other, but essentially, fundamentally, and unequivocally all of each other. We all need a drive for education and community as well as an insistence on an apostolic understanding of the faith. We all might like to believe that the activity of the Holy Spirit will inerrantly confer on us a right understanding, but all we need do is look around at the vast varieties of scriptural interpretation to appreciate that we all "see through a glass darkly." Our understanding always falls short of the truth of God. We need each other in community to help us discern this truth more clearly. I hope by the time we finish this discussion of the community of faith, we will not only appreciate some theology and ecclesiology concerning community, but also see some extremely important opportunities and reasons for ecumenism—the basis for the rejoining of the wondrous color palette of legitimate Christian expressions.

20

THE CURRENT CONTEXT

The Christian religion with all of its variations is a product of two thousand years of living out the tension between that which is eternally constant and that which is temporally new. As the guardian of the deposit of faith, the Church (however you may understand it) has a responsibility to its members to teach the essentials of the faith and to guide them in the way they live out this faith in their respective families, communities, nations, and the larger world. The passing on of the authentic apostolic teaching was Paul's central concern as he formed and guided the Gentile communities. The challenge is that while the Christian faith is at some level quite simple—Jesus Christ as the model for our lives—the deeper understanding, or at least appreciation, is more challenging. The Incarnation and the Paschal (Easter) Mystery that allows one to act out the simple part, requires not only study and learning, but also guidance and practice. We must not think that we can make this journey on our own. Not only do we need the grace of God received through the Church practices (for Anglicans, Lutherans, and

Catholics these would center on the sacraments) and the on-going activity of Christ and the Holy Spirit in our lives, but we also need a community of faith—a group of like-minded disciples of Christ who are on the same journey and who can lend support, love, and guidance as we practice and grow in our faith.

The current dilemma is that many Christian parishioners and pastors think that attending a worship service once a week is the minimum requirement for being a "good Christian." If one wants more, one can attend a Bible study, book study group, or even a specific group that practices one of the rich forms of Christian spirituality. While these latter opportunities certainly enrich one's life in Christ, they cannot take the place of a true community of faith that not only worships together, but also travels the road toward fullness in Christ together. These communal forms may lead to true community of faith, but they do not inherently have this scope or depth without some deliberate tweaking. Most Christians see these additional programs as just that—additional programs—which one participates in if he or she has the time and/or inclination. They do not see them as essential and integral parts of their Christian life.

Within the context of our inclination to develop programs around a central worship experience, we see some new phenomena arising: consolidated parishes, the mega-church, renewal movements, the charismatic movement, and the rise of small faith groups. Each of these has implications for our search for the authentic community of faith. The consolidation of parishes is seen not only in Catholic communities in larger cities and towns, but also in Protestant communities that may attract large numbers of members because of location, dynamic leadership, or style of worship. The reduction in the number of parishioners as well as the decline in the number of clergy has forced many of the smaller Catholic parishes to close and consolidate into much larger congregations of several thousand families. Instead of building large church structures that can accommodate these combined congregations, many parishes, both Catholic and Protestant, offer multiple services. A not-uncommon schedule might be a service on Saturday evening (especially for Catholics) and services at 7:30 a.m., 9:30 a.m., 11:30 a.m., and 5:00 p.m. on Sunday. While large parishes have the advantage of being able to offer a wide variety of opportunities for parishioners to participate in programs of different kinds, the challenge is clear that large parishes reduce intimacy. In many New England towns in the early 1900s one might have found several neighborhood parishes whose members all knew each other. Their children went to school together and played together. Families often visited informally after the worship service. Husbands and wives belonged to other groups within the parish that reinforced these natural connections. With the advent of much larger consolidated parishes, this natural intimacy was lost and many pastors were faced with the challenge of developing the intimacy of a community of faith within an inherently impersonal environment.

A second phenomenon that has burst onto the Christian scene is the advent of the mega-church. The roots of this phenomenon can be traced to the rise of charismatic conservative Protestant preachers such as Jerry Falwell, founder of the Thomas Road Baptist Church in Lynchburg, Virginia in 1956, which currently has a membership of over 24,000 under the leadership of his son, Jonathan. Charles Stanley is pastor of the First Baptist Church of Atlanta, which currently has 16,000 members. Radio and, even more so, television have greatly influenced the access of these preachers to wider audiences that ultimately may be attracted into full membership in their respective churches. Rick Warren's Saddleback Church in Lake Forest, California has a current congregation numbering 25,000 members. Joel Osteen's Lakewood Church in Houston, Texas, the largest church in the United States, currently has 44,000 members. Many of the newer mega-churches are considered to be non-denominational and stress lessons to be learned from the pastor's direct interpretation of Scripture. The experience of worship in a mega-church is usually centered on the pastor's message, as well as the musical and prayer environment. Because those who attend do so simply because they are searching for some tangible experience of the faith, worship tends to be lively with an enthusiastic participation of all present. While there may be numerous opportunities for Bible study or other programs, the communal nature of the faith is not central to these churches by their very size. Furthermore, evangelists and particularly televangelists such as Billy Graham, Robert Schuller, and Charles Stanley went far to disengage the message from the community. Many whose Christian journey was based on a television or radio sermon had little opportunity to delve more deeply into the nature of the community of faith. The Gospel or Good News seemed to be drifting away from that expressed by a primitive community of believers who shared not only their values and goals, but also their lives, toward a more intellectual understanding of basic truths without the context of the community to support and express them.

Renewal movements have arisen ever since the Church was formed. As a matter of fact, one might suggest that all new innovations to the faith have their roots in some sense of the need for renewal. These movements are based on the perception that old practices and ideologies have gone stale, and new concepts need to be implemented to renew vitality again. This attitude is not necessarily bad, although it has in many cases led to major deviations from apostolic traditions that are held by the "center" to be dangerous. What we are concerned with here are those movements that, while in accord with orthodox teachings (however you might like to define that), see a need to energize our appreciation of those teachings and how we live them out. One example of such a renewal movement is Cursillo, or a "small course" in Christianity. Begun in many Spanish Catholic churches in the 1940s, it spread to other countries and to other denominations, often under different names such as Walk to Emmaus and Via de Christo. It usually involves a three-day course in which talks are given on such topics as prayer, healing, and evangelism with lively discussion among participants and leaders. Practical aspects of Cursillo involve the care and treatment of the participants by the leaders in such a way that all get an experience of the love of Christ. Healing services and spiritual direction can be important parts of opening participants to aspects of their faith to which they may not have been exposed. The love and joy manifest is often transformative, and this transformation is further encouraged among members in weekly and monthly follow-up meetings. Clearly, Cursillo is a legitimate attempt to get at some of the essential aspects of a community of faith.

Another movement, founded by the Quaker Richard Foster, is Renovaré (since it is from the Latin "to renew," we should not need the accent, but they put it in for those of us who might want to pronounce it to rhyme with "Frigidaire.") From their vision statement we get: "We imagine a world in which people's lives flourish as they increasingly

become like Jesus."[81] They do this through interdenominational conferences, workshops, written materials, and
monthly "Conversations" in which interested participants
come together to learn from a speaker on a certain topic and
enter into dialogue concerning the meaning of the theme for
their lives. When I have attended these Conversations, I must
admit that I often feel more like I am in a true community
of faith than I do in my own parish. There is something very
powerful about the extra effort people must make to pay the
modest fee and to come out on a Saturday morning to attend.
The common interest and goal changes the whole dynamic
of the gathering from one of obligation to one of thirst—in
which everyone is somehow involved in feeding each other.
Attendance is restricted to no more than twenty-five participants, so discussion is possible and diversity is assured. The
common link is a desire to learn how the love of Christ is
expressed from various perspectives—such as an Episcopal
view of the value of the Desert Fathers, a Presbyterian view
of Julian of Norwich, and a Quaker view of the process of
discernment in community. While the specific topic of the
Conversations may be the initial impetus for participation,
ultimately the sharing that takes place seems to be more important and a clear indication of the power of the community
of faith to transcend denominational boundaries.

   The modern charismatic movement finds its roots in the
Pentecostalism of the early twentieth century—an expression of Christianity centered on the activity of the Holy
Spirit within the community of faith. It seems to have gotten its stronger impetus among Protestants and Catholics in
the early to mid-1960s, and it is often characterized by healing, speaking in tongues, prophesying, and the discernment

81 This statement can be found at http://www.renovare.org/about/vision.

of spirits. Because most mainstream Christian churches had moved away from such ecstatic expressions, charismatic Christians are often viewed with some suspicion as being overly emotional and irrational. It is interesting to look back over the history of the early Church and note the movement led by Montanus that took place somewhere around AD 150. It was also based upon the idea that the Holy Spirit was still active and could be manifest in ecstatic prophesy. The main problem was that Montanus elevated himself to a level that was inconsistent with the teachings of the larger Church— but the basic concept is still alive and well.

Because of the misunderstanding that often surrounds the charismatic movement, let me dwell here a bit. My first recollection of being confronted with someone who was clearly operating on a "higher spiritual level" was during prayer time at what is known as an Ultrea—a monthly meeting for those in designated regions of the state who had completed a Cursillo weekend. Steve was across the room with his hands up in the air, reaching for the sky in a state of ecstasy. As I was distracted from my own meager prayerful state by his gyrations, I could not help but scoff: "Really, Steve, you can't possibly be serious. This is way over the top and is bordering on the ridiculous." At that point (and I am not so advanced in my spiritual journey to have regular conversations with God) I heard a still small voice saying to me, "Jonny (the affectionate diminutive), you let *me* worry about Steve. You have enough to do to worry with Jonny." At that point I realized that I was not equipped to judge what Steve was up to, maybe he was further along in his spiritual journey than I was. I needed to concern myself with my own journey.

My second exposure came on a Tuesday evening when Kathryn Larisey and I were visiting a black church called

Abundant Life Outreach Ministries, whose pastor was a dynamic lady named Cynthia de Berry Freeman. At one point in the worship service, she said, "If you want to be saved and receive the Holy Ghost, rest on your feet." My first thought was that I certainly did not need to be saved. I had been baptized in the Episcopal Church when an infant. I had been confirmed. I had attended many different churches (see Part I) and was active in each one of them. Certainly she was not referring to *me*. Ok, well here is that still small voice again saying to me, "Jonny, would you do this for me?" *Hmmm,* well OK, but first I need to know what "rest on your feet" means, at which point someone stood up. *Got it!* So I stood up. Kathryn, not to be left out of the action, stood too. Cynthia reassured us that we would not be asked to "fall out"[82] or "foam at the mouth."

Sister Perry took us to a back room where we were "ministered to." We first read the part of Paul's letter to the Romans in which he says, ". . . if you confess with your lips that Jesus is Lord and believe in your heart that God raised him from the dead, you will be saved" (Rom 10:9). We all agreed, and with that we were declared to be *saved*. We then read a section from Paul's First Letter to the Corinthians in which he talks about receiving the Holy Spirit. Sister Perry then said that she would begin to pray in the Spirit—that is, to pray in tongues—which to most of us would just sound like gibberish—and that we should join in as we were moved to do so. I recall she was holding my hands, so I closed my eyes, rocked back on my heels and took a deep breath, at which point she shook my hands and said that I did not have to do

---

82 Some call this being "slain in the Spirit." It may appear to onlookers as a sort of swoon in which the person simply falls to the floor as he or she is being prayed over. It is often part of a healing prayer.

all that. I could just relax. *Hmmm, maybe there is something to this that I don't quite get yet.* Well, the upshot of it all was that I managed to utter what seemed to me to be gibberish while feeling utterly self-conscious. At that point it dawned on me that if I could get that self-consciousness out of the way, I might actually be able to utter sounds that came directly from the heart and thereby *pray in the Spirit.* In other words, my failure seemed to open the door to a deeper appreciation of what was possible. Cynthia passed away from cancer a few years ago, but I must thank her (and I suspect she is listening) for helping this white boy on his spiritual journey.

My last experience came when I attended a Life in the Spirit workshop at St. Mark Catholic Church in Clarkesville, Georgia, which was offered by admittedly charismatic Catholics in our parish. We spent the first part of the morning listening to talks about prayer and the way the Holy Spirit can influence our journey in Christ. The grand finale was a prayer service in the church. There were several "stations" where folks would pray over you if you desired. I was sitting in a pew next to my newfound spiritual friend, Carol Grasso, watching the proceedings and wondering whether I really wanted to participate. When there was no one in line at the station of Steve Dunlap, he came over to the station where his wife, Anne, was praying. I was totally enveloped by the love and complete presence they both exhibited as Anne prayed over her husband. OK, that did it. I decided to jump in, so I went to one of the other stations and at some point in the prayer found myself on the floor. This process is also known as "resting in the Spirit," and I really prefer that term, because that is really what is going on. You are so infused with peace that the most natural thing in the world to do is to *rest.* There is always someone behind you just in case that happens, but the more you are able to relax into the prayer the more likely you are to rest. When the service was over I remember one of the leaders, Pauline Dorman, said to me, "Wasn't that awesome?" My response was a bit surprising even to me. I said, "Actually, Pauline, it felt like normal life in the Spirit." In other words, it felt like the kind of life we are called to live every moment of every day as we surrender our lives to Christ and allow the Holy Spirit to infuse all of who we are and what we do. (Try not to "rest" while you are walking, jogging, swimming, or driving, however.) It was not so much "awesome" as "normal." I think at that point I had a newfound appreciation for a healthy and well-grounded charismatic dimension and what it can bring to our lives and our communities of faith. I'm not there yet, whatever that might mean, but I think I get the idea.

Finally, we might discuss three approaches that address the growing anonymity in modern large parishes and even many small ones. One of these movements is the growth of small faith groups or faith-sharing groups. These can be organized by the parish or can be formed informally by friends who seek a richer experience of their faith. They tend to be anywhere from five to ten people who see themselves on a common journey. They might be organized around a study of the Bible or the reading of other Christian texts and involve a rich discussion of the major themes of the reading, a sharing of related life experiences and struggles, and an open and often more charismatic prayer life. Members of such groups see sharing and prayer as fundamental aspects of the group—sharing their lives in a way that informs all present and prayer for each other, prayer for those outside the group, and prayer for certain specific issues that might arise in the life of the group, the church, the town, or the nation. Small faith groups allow for intimacy and transparency as members get to know and trust one another. There usually is a covenant that what is shared in the group stays in the group, so members will not go "sharing" about someone else's marriage trials, an instance of a sexually transmitted disease, or a propensity to dabble in pornography. You can see how such sharing could be both healing and at the same time very destructive, if trust were not an integral part of the group. Some churches believe that the answer to community is to be found in these groups.[83]

Another approach to the dissolution of true community in the Catholic Church is what is known as the Neocatechumenal Way. They often call themselves The Way, but others now referred to them as NeoCats. Originating in Spain in 1964, the Neocatechumenal Way is designed for the ongoing formation of adults in the Catholic faith, but is much more centered on a communal experience rather than simply on catechesis or instruction. Its three guiding principles include Scripture, liturgy and community and involve an effort to lead participants toward fraternal communion and mature faith. In fact, one might assert that their approach implies that there is no mature faith without fraternal communion.

The expressions of this approach are based in existing parishes and yet create a different environment in which worship and community are combined. These parish-based communities are comprised of twenty to fifty members. The most dramatic difference from traditional Catholicism is found in their style of worship. The Eucharist (Holy Communion) is celebrated in small groups with participants seated around a

83 See Michael White and Tom Corcoran, *Rebuilt* (Notre Dame, Ind.: Ave Maria Press, 2013) for a discussion of how they used small faith groups to help build community.

table. Each of the Scripture readings is preceded by a substantial "monition" or instruction offered by one of the participants and followed by a number of "echoes," or "resonances," offered by any of those present. The latter are personal reflections on the meaning of the scriptural passage for their lives. The priest's homily is then added to the resonances, but tends to be more in the line of hermeneutics or preaching. Communion is taken in banquet form, whereby the consecrated bread is broken and distributed to those present as they remain seated and the wine is distributed to each one present by the priest. In other words, it looks a lot more like a family dinner than the normal Catholic mass. As you can see, the way Scripture and liturgy are interrelated demonstrates the emphasis on community. In other words, the way Scripture is expounded within the liturgy is inherently communal.

This movement has not developed without its critics, however. Many see it as divisive within a parish, separating those who *are* from those who *are not*. Many also see the liturgical variants being introduced to be in conflict with the norms of the Catholic Church, and as one might imagine, norms are important to Catholics. In their defense, one might see the struggle for authentic Christian community as absolutely valid. One can understand the desire for establishing patterns of behavior that enhance the fabric of community that otherwise might be missing from the normal Catholic parish life. Like the charismatic movement, many view the Neocatechumenal Way with suspicion. It is easy to be suspect of something of which you are not a part. The challenge might be to see the verities that are being expressed and try to capture those within the traditional Catholic, or even Protestant, parish setting in such a way that division is not necessary.

In this context, we might say that a third community-building mechanism is possibly most important because it can exist within the current church structure and need not be seen as anything but an extension of worship—Sunday school—both for children and adults. For Protestants, Sunday school is a no-brainer. As we have said, it is a way of life. For Catholics, however, we might just do a little explanation. Sunday school takes place, as you might have guessed, on Sunday in association with the worship service, either before or after. For churches with multiple services, the challenge is to place the Sunday school program in between the two largest services. Unfortunately, if there are three or more services, someone is left out. Adult Sunday school, which is our main focus here, is usually centered on some theme such as Bible study, a topic of interest, or a specific reading. Some are thematically organized, while some are organized by the age of the members. Some last for a certain number of weeks that will allow the exposition of the topic being treated, while others are a perpetual Bible study. Some are more lecture oriented, while some include discussion, but most at least give the participants an opportunity to meet other members of the parish in a more intimate setting and at least to learn their names. For some denominations, Sunday school is seen as "optional." For others, the tradition and culture is so strong that worship and Sunday school are inseparable. Sunday school may be the only place where parishioners learn Scripture, church doctrine, and church culture. Sunday school is where parishioners get to develop the kinds of loving relationships that are pointed toward in worship. For some denominations, Sunday school for adults does not exist. For other large congregations, traditional Sunday school has been abandoned in favor of some of the community-building mechanisms mentioned above. The trick here is to see the value of an interaction within the community of faith outside the worship service and to try to see our way clear to designing an experience that would allow the full flowering of the love of Christ.

21

A THEOLOGICAL PERSPECTIVE

Two primary questions of life are: *What are we doing here?* and *Why do we do what we do?* Is our purpose simply to assure ourselves of eternal life in heaven, or is there also something more immediate, more pressing—here and now? The central premise of any Christian community of faith is theological in nature. If we are called to a radical transformation into the perfect likeness of Jesus Christ *right now,* then this becomes our immediate goal.[84] If the Gospel, or the Good News, is that the eternal life of God has been made available to us *right now* through Jesus Christ, then how we live this out in the community of faith becomes central to why we are

---

84 The term "perfect" is used here to emphasize that we are not just called to be "closer" to Christ. All Christian denominations would assert this. The value of a more radical Christology is that it asserts that Christ offers *all* of himself to us. The term "perfect" is intended to remove any doubt or "wiggle room" concerning this understanding of the radical call to perfection in Christ. This idea is consistent with the Catholic tradition that every Christian is called to be an *alter Christus*—another Christ. Many Protestant traditions, such as the Wesleyans, are called "holiness" churches in that they profess the call of individuals into the holiness of Jesus Christ.

Christians. If the only "new commandment" that our Lord gave us was to "love one another as I have loved you" (John 13:34), then we must find a way within the context of parish life to reflect this absolute directive. If Jesus states very clearly that "everyone will know that you are my disciples, if you have love for one another" (John 13:35), then it is essential that we find a way to nurture this love within our parish community. If this deepest meaning of the Incarnation, the Paschal Mystery, and the teachings of our Lord is seen to be distinctly Christian, then we must, as faithful Christians, find a way to experience them, teach them, practice them, and evangelize them—both within and outside the parish church family—and we must have a good reason for doing so.

The Christian community of faith must address these fundamental theological perspectives by extending the experience of worship into the realm of action, growth, and ultimate transformation. As a professor of theology once said to me, "Don't go out and *follow* Jesus—go out and *be* Jesus." What he meant was that our transformation into the perfect likeness of Jesus Christ (whether or not it is completed in this life is not the point) was a transformation of *being*—not just of *action*. As medieval theologians would assert, action does not change until our being changes—action follows being—*agere sequitur esse*. Such a transformation does not take place outside a deeply committed community of faith in which other individuals and the Holy Spirit are active participants in both the individual and communal transformation process.

If we are to see the characteristics of the community of faith as a theological reality, then we must first understand what we mean by "theological." In its most basic form, theology is simply the study of God. Because there are many perspectives from which we can study God, there are many theologies. Systematic Theology, the broadest and most all-inclusive perspective looks at the nature of God in a systematic way from an historical as well as a conceptual perspective. It will intersect all the other more focused theological perspectives in some way. Biblical Theology stresses the evidence for our understanding of God from a purely biblical point of view. Sacramental Theology looks at the justification and meaning for the various sacraments, the outward signs of God's grace, such as baptism, the Lord's Supper, and marriage.[85] Trinitarian Theology looks at the biblical and conceptual basis for our understanding of God as threefold—Father, Son, and Holy Spirit—as well as its value in our practice of our Christian faith. Trinitarian Theology is particularly important in our understanding of the community of faith, because it sees God as essentially a community of three persons (not three "gods"). Moral Theology looks specifically at God as the source of our morality. This is particularly compelling from the point of view of the apparently different approaches taken to morality in the Old and New Testaments. Jesus clearly intended to enrich our understanding of our moral stands without diminishing their importance. Liberation Theology has been quite a controversial area ever since Gustavo Gutiérrez, a Peruvian Catholic priest, clearly articulated it in 1971 in his work *A Theology of Liberation*. Its emphasis was on Jesus as the savior to and for the poor and took its basis from biblical passages showing Jesus' concern for the poor and oppressed in the New Testament and leaning on liberation themes, such as the events of Exodus, in the Hebrew Bible. Aesthetic Theology, advanced by the Catholic theologian Hans Urs von

---

85 Others would add any or all of the sacraments of ordination, reconciliation, confirmation, and anointing of the sick. As we well know, the decision of which sacraments are essential often defines a major difference between the various Christian denominations.

Balthasar, stressed the relationship of our understanding of and sensibility toward beauty as a central organizing principle for our understanding of and sensibility toward God. We could continue, but you get the picture—there are as many theologies as there are perspectives. Each perspective sheds its own new light on the challenge of understanding who God is and how he influences our lives.

In this vast panorama of theological perspectives, we might define a theology of community. Some important Catholic and Eastern Orthodox contributors in the area include Dennis Doyle, [86] Joseph Ratzinger, [87] Henri de Lubac, [88] Ives Congar, [89] Jean-Marie Tillard, [90] Avery Dulles, [91] John Zizioulas, [92] and Miroslav Volf. [93] Protestants who have made significant contributions include Howard Snyder, [94] Tom Sine, [95] Shane Claiborne, [96] and Stanley Grenz. [97] While it is beyond the

86 Dennis M. Doyle, *Communion Ecclesiology* (Maryknoll, New York: Orbis Books, 2000).

87 Joseph Ratzinger, *Called to Communion* (San Francisco: Ignatius Press, 1996).

88 Henri de Lubac, *The Splendor of the Church* (San Francisco: Ignatius Press, 1999).

89 Ives Congar, *Diversity and Communion* (London: SCM Press Ltd, 1984).

90 Jean-Marie Tillard, *Church of Churches: an Ecclesiology of Communion*, trans. R. G. DePeaux (Collegeville, Minnesota: Liturgical Press, 1992).

91 Avery Dulles, *Models of the Church* (New York: Doubleday, 2002).

92 John D. Zizioulas, *Being as Communion* (Crestwood, New York: St Vladimir's Seminary Press, 1985).

93 Miroslav Volf, *After Our Likeness: The Church as the Image of the Trinity* (Grand Rapids: Eerdmans, 1998).

94 Howard Snyder, *The Community of the King* (Downers Grove: InterVarsity Press, 2004), 89–137.

95 Tom Sine, *The New Conspirators* (Downers Grove: InterVarsity Press, 2008), 253–66.

96 Shane Claiborne, *The Irresistible Revolution* (Grand Rapids: Zondervan, 2006), 115–53.

97 Stanley J. Grenz, *Theology for the Community of God* (Grand Rapids: Eerdmans, 2000), 461–570.

scope of this effort to synthesize these contributions and articulate such a theology, we at least might point toward its possible form and substance. A theology of community must of course start with a theology of the nature of God that is essentially communal—the Trinity. As we discussed above, the Trinity informs not only the activity of the community of faith in terms of its relationship to the teachings and actions of Jesus Christ in the Incarnation, but also the understanding of how the Holy Spirit informs that activity in terms of prayer. The nature of the relationship between the Father and Son informs our relationships among members of the community, and the nature of Jesus himself informs the depth of the transformation that is the central goal of the community. But the Trinity also informs the structure of the community of faith and its relationship to other aspects of church life—the very centrality of community in God implies a centrality of community within the Christian Church and its associated congregations.

From an elucidation of the Trinity as a wellspring, one would then look at biblical evidence for the importance of community in the early Israelite understanding of its relationship to God and God's directives toward relationships among the members of the community of believers. It is not hard to see that, while there certainly are commandments that concern things other than human relationships, the central ones, particularly as seen in the Ten Commandments, are all about relationships between God and humanity and among humanity. The fact that the Hebrew Bible is basically a set of stories about relationships unequivocally asserts that God's way is mostly about salvation within the community and not simply individual salvation. Furthermore, the meaning of these stories and associated relationships were always interpreted in terms of the Hebrew community. If God was pleased with the community, then the community flourished. If God was displeased, then the community experienced slavery, exile, floods, and the admonition of the prophets to change its ways.

It is an easy step from the fundamentals of how the members of the Hebrew community were to relate to one another (e.g. don't steal from one another, don't mess around with someone else's wife, etc.) to those that were articulated by Jesus Christ in the New Testament community of disciples and that were carried on in the early Christian communities that evolved. While loving God and neighbor were well known concepts in the Hebrew Scripture, Jesus elevates them to the "summary of the Law." And not only does he elevate the love of neighbor, but also the love of *enemy*:[98]

> You have heard that it was said, 'You shall love your neighbor and hate your enemy.' But I say to you, Love your enemies and pray for those who persecute you . . . (Matt 5:43–44)

In other words, the centerpiece of the Christian life is love—and love is relational. If God is love and love is relational, then we don't really need to take a great leap to arrive at the conclusion that the life of the Church and particularly the lives of individual parishes or congregations must essentially be communal. Once we establish this theologically, we are challenged to work it out in practice within an ecclesial or church setting.

---

98 We should point out that Jesus is not saying that the Old Testament said that one should hate one's enemies. In fact, Prov 25:21 states, "If your enemy is hungry, give him bread to eat; and if he is thirsty, give him water to drink." He is elevating rather than inventing.

22

AN ECCLESIAL PERSPECTIVE

While we might have a high-minded theological justification for the centrality of the community of faith
as an essential aspect of our lives as followers of Jesus Christ,
such a manifestation must be worked out within the context of the Church, whether it is Catholic, mainline Protestant, Orthodox, or Evangelical. This means that the particular form of the community of faith must be consistent with
the culture of the larger Church body. One of the important
starting points in any discussion of the relationship between
the larger Church body and any related community of faith
would be what has been termed *communion ecclesiology*. This
means the study of community within the context of the *ec-
clesia* or church.[99]

One theologian who continually raises the theme of

---

99 See Dennis Doyle, *Communion Ecclesiology* (Maryknoll, New York: Orbis
Books, 2000). Dennis Doyle has made an important contribution in this
area. His study focuses on an exposition of and commentary on a wide
range of theologians regarding their understanding of the role of communion within the Church. Its major value is a most generous and insightful
overview of the issue and an introduction to a vast array of resources.

community is Joseph Ratzinger, Pope Benedict XVI. In his work *Introduction to Christianity*, he repeatedly makes bold statements regarding the fact that Christianity is essentially communal in nature.

> Ultimately religion is not to be found along the solitary path of the mystic, but only in the community of proclaiming and hearing. Man's conversation with God and men's conversation with one another are mutually necessary and interdependent.[100]

While the history of the Church is full of important contributions to the spiritual life by mystics, the essence of religion, not just faith in all its various forms, is essentially communal. In other words, there can be no effective Christianity without a community of faith. In a sense, this takes us back to the historical context in which we discussed the essential role the apostles played in the Christ event. No apostles, no effective Incarnation. Now this may appear to be an overreaching statement, but from a purely logistical point of view this kind of necessary relationship exists all around us. If we are talking about the value of an item to a seller, without a buyer there is no market, no price, and no value to the item. If we are talking about a lover, if there is no beloved there is no actual love. In other words, it takes two to tango. A person cannot, by definition, tango by themselves, and we could just as fruitfully assert that a person cannot be a lover by themselves, a seller cannot make a market by themselves, and most especially the Christ cannot be the Christ by himself. Jesus needed to express the nature of the new covenant

---

100 Ratzinger, *Introduction to Christianity*, 95.

not only as a relationship between man and God, but also
between man and man. One cannot love God, whom he has
not seen, unless he loves his neighbor, whom he has seen.[101]
Even many of the mystics were in some form of community,
but while the solitary aspect of their lives was fruitful, it was
not sufficient for their lives as Christians.

One angle Pope Benedict takes is a discussion on freedom. He first makes the case that freedom in the Greek sense
of the word did not primarily refer to the ability to make
alternative decisions or choose alternative actions, but was
grounded in the full membership of a citizen in the state—
one who not only participated fully in the life of the state,
but also had responsibility for that life and thus could access
a set of concomitant rights and privileges that accrue to him
as a result of that membership. The ultimate right in such a
state is the right to reach one's full potential as a citizen in the
context of the state. In other words, freedom was inconceivable outside the larger communal context in which it was
acted out.[102]

Finally, John Paul II in his Apostolic Letter, *Novo Millennio Inuente*, contemplates the concrete plans he envisions
for the new millennium. In section IV, entitled "Witness to
Love," he writes a dense apologetic for communion:

> 42. "By this all will know that you are my disci-
> ples, if you have love for one another" (*Jn* 13:35).
>
> If we have truly contemplated the face of Christ,
> dear Brothers and Sisters, our pastoral plan-
> ning will necessarily be inspired by the "new

---

101 See 1 John 4:20.
102 Ratzinger, *Church, Ecumenism, and Politics*, 190–191.

commandment" which he gave us: "Love one another, as I have loved you" (*Jn* 13:34).

This is the other important area in which there has to be commitment and planning on the part of the universal Church and the particular Churches: *the domain of communion (koinonia),* which embodies and reveals the very essence of the mystery of the Church. Communion is the fruit and demonstration of that love which springs from the heart of the Eternal Father and is poured out upon us through the Spirit which Jesus gives us (cf. *Rom* 5:5), to make us all "one heart and one soul" (*Acts* 4:32). It is in building this communion of love that the Church appears as "sacrament", as the "sign and instrument of intimate union with God and of the unity of the human race."[103]

43. To make the Church *the home and the school of communion*: that is the great challenge facing us in the millennium which is now beginning, if we wish to be faithful to God's plan and respond to the world's deepest yearnings.

But what does this mean in practice? Here too, our thoughts could run immediately to the action to be undertaken, but that would not be the right impulse to follow. Before making practical plans, we need *to promote a spirituality of communion,*

103 Second Vatican Ecumenical Council, Dogmatic Constitution on the Church *Lumen Gentium*, 1.

making it the guiding principle of education
wherever individuals and Christians are formed,
wherever ministers of the altar, consecrated persons, and pastoral workers are trained, wherever
families and communities are being built up. A
spirituality of communion indicates above all the
heart's contemplation of the mystery of the Trinity dwelling in us, and whose light we must also
be able to see shining on the face of the brothers
and sisters around us. A spirituality of communion also means an ability to think of our brothers and sisters in faith within the profound unity of the Mystical Body, and therefore as "those
who are a part of me." This makes us able to
share their joys and sufferings, to sense their desires and attend to their needs, to offer them deep
and genuine friendship.[104]

These concepts point unequivocally toward the building
of the Christian community of faith within the context of
the larger Church (however you may define that)—a concrete expression of the Christian understanding of our call
to be transformed into the perfect likeness of Jesus Christ,
which itself cannot be understood outside of our relationships
of love toward others.[105]

---

104 John Paul II, *Novo Millennio Inuente* (2000), www.vatican.va, apostolic
letters.

105 For those of you who are not Catholic, I am not suggesting that these
statements by Benedict and John Paul are "gospel" merely because they are
Popes, but they are true because they are in accord with the whole Christ
event and articulate far better than I the foundation on which all of us
Christians must build the Christian experience in our own times and in our
own congregations.

How does this process of community building work it-self out within a larger institutional Church setting? There are several ways in which Church structure influences com-munity and community influences Church structure. As we are well aware, there is a wide range of Church "polities" or political structures represented in the various Christian de-nominations. The Catholic Church would typify a highly hi-erarchical structure with the pope at the top, bishops running regional "churches", and priests running local parishes. Col-legiality is present and practiced, but the structure allows for a higher level of control than in more congregational systems. The way in which bishops see their roles as pastors to priests, and priests see their role as pastors to members of their con-gregations often is reflective of the way in which the larger Church body is structured. Structures in which collegiality is emphasized can at least point toward the development of this same kind of collegiality at all levels of Church structure.

Let me offer an example. The following is a profound prayer from St. Ignatius of Loyola:

> *Take, Lord, and receive all my liberty,*
> *my memory, my understanding*
> *and my entire will,*
> *All I have and call my own.*
> *You have given all to me.*
> *To you, Lord, I return it.*
> *Everything is yours; do with it what you will.*
> *Give me only your love and your grace.*
> *That is enough for me.*[106]

---

106 This prayer can be found at http://www.bc.edu/bc_org/prs/stign/ prayers.html, accessed on December 3, 2013.

Notice that it is basically the prayer of an individual—a powerful acknowledgement of one's relationship to God. I am not implying that this prayer does not reflect fundamental truths. I have often thought, however, that there is one little point that is missing in the last line that would transform it into a communally-oriented prayer:

> *Give me only your love and your grace* and someone
> to share it with.
> *That is enough for me.*

It is funny how we often miss these little parts of the puzzle and think that what we are doing is only between God and ourselves as individuals. The way we pray is often influenced by the way we see ourselves within the larger ecclesial structure of which we are a part.

Baptist churches, on the other hand, exhibit a congregational polity in which the local congregation has control over leadership and programs. This local control requires a level of cooperation among members of the congregation that can point toward a communal spirit of shared authority and responsibility.

The reverse, although less likely, may also be true: a sense of community can influence the way a larger church body is structured. Because the development of structure occurs early in a denomination's formation, the prevailing understanding of the nature of the Christian walk will influence the way leaders see their goals and the options available to them for achieving those goals. If community is seen as an essential goal, then worship, education, and other programs will be viewed as expressions of the community of faith. If, on the other hand, church leaders see the essential nature of the Christian walk as manifest in one's individual relationship to God, then worship, education, and other programs will be structured quite differently.

Liturgies that are found in liturgical churches such as the Episcopalians, the Lutherans, the Eastern Orthodox, and the Catholics are established by those outside the local congregation. These liturgies can be influenced by the perceptions of Church leadership and can have a significant impact on the way members of a congregation see themselves in relation to each other. The old Catholic Latin mass, in which the congregation is operating more as an observer, looks very different from a communal standpoint than the modern Catholic mass replete with spoken and sung responses.

The current Catholic prayer of confession is an example of liturgical influence:

> *I confess to almighty God*
> *and to you, my brothers and sisters,*
> *that I have greatly sinned,*
> *in my thoughts and in my words,*
> *in what I have done*
> *and in what I have failed to do,*
> *through my fault, through my fault,*
> *through my most grievous fault;*
> *therefore I ask blessed Mary ever-Virgin,*
> *all the Angels and Saints,*
> *and you, my brothers and sisters,*
> *to pray for me to the Lord our God.*

Aside from the place Mary plays in your worship (if you are of a Protestant bent), my point has to do with the inclusion of the words "my brothers and sisters." At some point, rather recently, the Catholic Church wanted to articulate clearly the communal nature of our relationship to one another. The inclusion of these words is obviously an attempt to broaden one's understanding of the shared relationships we have within the community of faith. It is through such changes in wording that larger liturgical churches can influence their congregation's perception of their communal nature. Church leadership, thus, can be influenced by their shared understanding of community and, thereby, make adjustments to Church structure and practices that reflect that understanding. These changes at the ecclesial level can then have a strong influence on perceptions at the parish level.

We would be remiss if we didn't talk about the interface between communities of faith and Church theology. It was clear from the very beginning that the major concern for the apostles was that they would pass on to others a correct understanding of what happened when Jesus of Nazareth lived, preached, died, was resurrected from the dead, and ascended into Heaven. One of the important roles of the larger ecclesial bodies is to carry on this role of guarding the apostolic tradition. The good news about hierarchical churches is that they have a better chance of fulfilling this responsibility. The not-so-good news is that they may also be so bogged down in this hierarchy that they lose that sense of intimate collegiality that is essential for an authentic community of faith to flourish. The reverse might be said of churches in which individual congregations have more control. They may have more difficulty in "vetting" the teachings of the pastor or the congregation leadership, but may also be more inclined to understand their lives together as communal in nature. Finding the balance may be the job of the larger ecclesial bodies.

One final way in which church structure influences

community is in its decision-making process. It might be fruitful to envision how the Christ event might have worked itself out differently if the Synagogue leadership had been less hierarchical and more communal in nature. Would the Pharisees have been less threatened? Would they have sat down with him and tried to discern whether the Spirit of God was working mightily in him? The same challenge might be true for us. If Jesus showed up today in one of our churches and suggested a more communal form of worship, Sunday school, food bank, or soup kitchen, would he be welcomed, heard, and responded to? Remember, he would have no credentials, no black shirt and collar (and certainly no purple shirt and pectoral cross) as a sign of his authority, and no position of importance in the Church hierarchy. As far as the ecclesial body is concerned, he would be a big *nobody*. Would we be able to recognize him? This question might be a good mental benchmark against which to view our Church structures and how responsive they might be to Jesus himself. We might put it another way: how are our gatherings of Christians—both parishes and congregations which we like to call communities—open to the movement of the Holy Spirit through the relationships that are formed in accord with the admonition to love one another as Christ loved us—the Eleventh Commandment? Has our larger ecclesial body created rigid structures that preclude the possibility of such movement? Are we so constrained by authority that the love of Christ cannot be learned and acted out? The overarching question being posed here is: How can our ecclesial bodies be facilitators of community at the parish level?

23

A PAROCHIAL PERSPECTIVE

Parishes are complex gatherings of—you guessed it—a wide variety of parishioners—folks who for an equally wide variety of reasons show up at church on Sunday morning. Some might be seeking serene comfort in a highly liturgical setting. Others could want simply to be left alone to sit on the back pew, quietly allowing the spirituality of the service to flow over them and wash away their anxieties. Some are searching for the fellowship of like-minded folks. Others might be looking for a meaningful and real experience of faith within a worship service in which all participants are excited to be there and are seeking the same thing. Still others are seeking a much simpler experience of the movement of the Holy Spirit. We could go on and on. Each Christian tradition offers a slightly different kind of worship experience, all of which have some important validity. Furthermore, each of us comes to those experiences with a host of noble and not-so-noble motives. The simplicity of the Baptists is important as it reminds us that God is not about trappings. The glorious liturgy and beautiful worship spaces of the Catholics is equally important as it points toward the glory of God and that God is worthy of our adoration in words and art. In other words, the main point may have much less to do with our style of worship than our *style of love.*

What might we mean by the concept *style of love*? We are really pointing toward the love of Christ. As we have said, this love is very different from the love of country, the love of a friend, or the love of a spouse—although all of these are changed as they incorporate the love that Christ showed us. It is this love that we are striving to define as we clarify our understanding of the community of faith.

This love can be manifest in the way we approach everything we do. On the other hand, it can be ignored in the way we approach everything we do. We can study Scripture to enhance our understanding of Scripture or we can study Scripture to enhance our understanding of the love of Christ. We may enhance our ability to love by solitary prayer through which the Holy Spirit fills our hearts with love. If we, however, use solitary prayer time as an escape from the "demands" of love, we have missed the point. If we bask in the incredible beauty of the Sistine Chapel but have not love, we are a "noisy gong or a clanging cymbal" (1 Cor 13:1), and if we have memorized all of Paul's letter to the Romans and have not love, we are "nothing" (1 Cor 13:2). That sort of puts the whole thing into perspective. "Nothing" is as low as you can go. It is even lower than a noisy gong. Love is not only the name of this "game"—it is the *only* game.

Parishes are the places where community is built—or not built, as the case may be. Parishes can be places where superficial relationships are maintained or places where true intimate community is fostered. Parishes are the places where apparently meaningful activities absorb all our time so that real community building *cannot* take place, or they can be places where opportunities are deliberately structured such that consistent community building *does* take place.

The reality, however, is that many parishes face challenges: complex worship schedules, a culture of members "bouncing" from one service to another according to one's personal convenience, the lack of bricks and mortar that form meeting spaces, and the lack of a culture that encourages the linkage between worship and more personal intimate gatherings that allow relationships to be formed and love to be manifest. Often these challenges pose apparently insurmountable obstacles to the process of developing a viable community of faith.

One of the challenges in the American Church may be a limitation on physical resources and clergy, which leads to fewer parishes and multiple worship services. While multiple services may be a sign of desirable growth, two consequences arise: the perception that one service is just as good as another and the logistics of when to schedule community-building functions so that the greatest number can participate. The multiplicity of "options" for a parishioner has given the impression that these options, if not intended to do so, can be accessed according to their "convenience." The result is that the constituency of any given service is constantly changing, not unlike a drive-in movie theater. The challenge for the community-building process is to devise a vehicle that is consistent with this reality, but at the same time has the capacity to draw the parish toward a new and richer concept of "community of faith." Not unlike the Incarnation, the vehicle must meet us where we are and at the same time be capable of taking us somewhere closer to God.

Any gathering of the community of faith at one time on a Sunday morning would suit only a portion of the congregation. If existing Sunday school classes are seen as such a vehicle, the complexity of the worship schedule precludes the possibility of having, for example, one Sunday school class "between services" that meets the needs of all parishioners. There are just too many "betweens." Thus we might have to consider that a community-building effort, if it is to be connected to the worship service, should be implemented before or after a given worship service. Ultimately the effort, if successful, would have such an opportunity associated with *every* service. In other words, the concept is that the community experience would ultimately become a part of the total worship "package." The gathering of the community of faith would therefore include worship as an encounter with Christ in prayer, preaching, liturgy, and song, as well as an encounter with Christ in each other through dialogue, leaning, sharing, etc.

The problem of bricks and mortar is an interesting challenge that is viewed quite differently by our Catholic brethren and our Protestant brethren. As we discussed above, the Protestant tradition is one based on the centrality of Scripture. As such, it assumes that everyone will be engaged in learning the Bible. Therefore, adult Sunday school spaces are provided for just this purpose. In general, we can say that Protestants tend to build more extensive "parish house" facilities. On the other hand, the tradition of educating children in the context of the faith is much stronger than adult education in the Catholic tradition, so it is not uncommon for a parochial school to be attached to a Catholic parish. Unfortunately, the bricks and mortar for schools is not as amenable as gathering spaces for community building as are "parish house" spaces. One related logistical challenge for Catholics is the fact that the children who go to Catholic school get their catechism training in school, while those who go to public or non-Catholic private schools must get that training on Sunday, or some other appropriate time. Thus, "Sunday school" for children is restricted to those children who do not go to Catholic schools. This tends to split the adult congregation into families who have children in Catholic schools and those who do not. And yet the community of faith should include everyone. Whatever is designed must somehow address these kinds of challenges.

Finally, we should talk about the linkage between worship and community building. Recall that in the early church, worship and community building were one and the same. As congregations grew and worship became more corporate and less personal, community building had to take place outside the worship service, if it were to happen at all. If you buy the idea that it is important to link worship and community building, then Sunday school as it now exists in many churches is the closest vehicle we have that is directly connected to our main worship services. As we have mentioned, this linkage is very strong among Baptists and Evangelicals, strong among some other mainline Protestant traditions, and weaker in the Catholic tradition. There is some good news and some not-so-good news regarding the Catholics. The good news is that because they do not have a strong Sunday school tradition, there possibly is not the same challenge to "change" what has been done before. The not-so-good news is that in many instances one might be starting from scratch to establish a new linkage that has never existed before.

Why have I not been stressing home churches and small faith sharing groups? Most simply, I could say that my gut tells me this is not the direction that will ultimately heal the break between corporate worship and the community of faith. Many feel that these more personal vehicles are the answer. I am simply building a case for one alternative and would ask the reader to follow me in this journey and see where it takes us.

All of these challenges must be seen in the context of the parish leadership and their willingness to forge a new pathway. Again, styles of leadership vary greatly among the different Christian traditions. Those traditions that exhibit a congregational polity, a structure that is centered on the congregation, will have a leadership that places more emphasis on the parish council, the vestry, or a bench of ruling elders. Those that exhibit a more hierarchical structure will have a leadership that places more emphasis on the church pastor. Every individual parish will exhibit a blend of these kinds of leadership styles based on their history and the strength of current personalities in leadership roles. The point here is that the implementation of a community-building effort will have to take into account a number of physical, cultural, and leadership issues. The politics of change, therefore, becomes a challenge in different parish settings. In some parishes merely the mention of the desire to try something new brings applause and encouragement from the leadership. In others, proposals must be written, submitted in triplicate and await sequential approval from a hierarchy of responsible "agents." Having the opportunity to try may depend on how one "plays the game." You may have to wait until a pastor retires, a director of Christian education passes into the larger life, or Hell freezes over before someone will say to you, "I think you are on the right track. Give it a try, and I will help you." We will talk much more about the actual implementation of such an effort in the next chapter.

24

CHRIST ENCOUNTER II

PROMPTINGS

Since you have read something of my own personal journey, you know of my spasmodic lurching from one denomination to another. When I finally became a Catholic, *I was committed*. I made up my mind that this was the end of the road—in a good sense. I would pitch my tent and make my fire here. If I needed to clear the land or plant a crop, I would do it here. If there were stars to gaze at and musings to be done, I would do it from here. Through my wanderings, I came to the singular realization that no one has all the answers. The Quakers may stress the personal experience of God only to run the risk of losing the ability to articulate a clear understanding of the person of Jesus Christ. The Catholics may preserve a hierarchical structure that allows them to struggle over two thousand years to achieve a priceless Christology at the risk of losing the lively activity of the Holy Spirit in the community of faith. Pentecostal Christians may stress the activity of the Holy Spirit and lose touch with the historic roots of the early Church. Bonhoeffer, by stressing the dangers of introducing human shortcomings into the concept of a Christian community of faith, runs the risk of turning the community-building effort into a pure abstraction. Fletcher, in an effort to make the community of faith a concrete reality may be running the risk of eliminating the importance of our personal journey and our individual relationship with God. In other words, there are traps everywhere one turns, but at some point one must just plant one's stake and work outward from there. The hope would be that no matter what our starting point, with thoughtful and prayerful effort, we just might come to the center of what Jesus would recognize as the Kingdom of God on Earth. We really do need the strengths of each other to find the integrity of the whole.

In light of the inherent limitations of only one point of view, these promptings have come from a Catholic perspective. But that need not have been the case. They could have come from any Christian perspective. The prompting challenges might have been different, but the overall challenge would have been the same—to create and experience the love of Christ as he intended for us to do. Some might be frustrated by an emphasis on intellectual issues and desire more spirituality. Some might be frustrated by an abundance of spirituality and desire more concrete ministry. Some might be frustrated by being lectured to all the time and desire more meaningful and creative dialogue. Some might be frustrated by too much dialogue and not enough authoritative teaching.

My perspective, being new in the Catholic Church, gave me a clean slate. I did not know what to expect, so as I encountered people, places, and culture, I had no preconceived notion of their meaning and worth. An example might be the first time I saw the Knights of Columbus, with their plumed hats, capes, and swords. My response was, *"Hmmm, what do you make of that?"* I was learning and had no basis for any value judgment. I may still be in that mode with regard to many customs in the Catholic Church, but here are a few observations that became promptings. During the process of becoming a Catholic, called the Rite of Christian Initiation for Adults, I was part of a group of about twenty folks all of whom were on the same journey. In other words, I was part of a community—I felt connected to the teachers and the participants. Once I was received into the Church in April of 2009, I found that there was no Sunday school for adults and, especially because I am single, this meant that I went to mass and went home. I did not know very many people in the larger parish, so life in my church suddenly became rather lonely. When I moved from Columbia, South Carolina to Clarkesville, Georgia, I had in the back of my mind to see if we could form some kind of regular communal experience after mass. After about a year, the parish was probably about ready to let me take a crack at it, but by that time I was ready to leave Clarkesville for Denver. When I started to attend St. Mary Parish in Littleton, my first task was to look up the Christian Education Coordinator and tell her what I wanted to do. I probably scared her to death, since neither she nor anyone else in the parish knew anything about me, but she was kind enough to suggest that I write a proposal and send it to her.

THE PROPOSAL

As you have seen, all my background and efforts had been pointing me toward some form of communal experience— one that would express a meaningful balance among all the various aspects of what I viewed as an authentic community of faith. From here on I will be offering *one* approach that was geared to *one* setting in an effort to address a unique set of challenges. Your challenges certainly will be different, but it could well be that your solution will look a lot like mine, if all the pieces of the communal puzzle are to work together. I hope the details of my effort will at least keep this whole enterprise from devolving into an abstract intellectual exercise. The challenge for all of us is to turn our understanding into something concrete. Whatever we do, the chances are it will be experimental and will need some tweaking and a lot of mutual generosity, patience, commitment, and prayer for it to bear fruit.

With this qualification let me tell you how I approached the challenge. My first task was to come up with a name for my effort that would capture the essence of what it was about. I thought of an experience I had at Sea World many years ago, called "Shark Encounter." Toward the end of the show we were led into a large Plexiglas tube that ran through the shark aquarium. We were literally surrounded by all kinds of sharks. It was stunning. We truly had an encounter with sharks in their own world. Somehow I wanted to have that same level of close encounter with Jesus Christ, and at this point I had in mind a kind of open-ended discussion group. I thought of calling it Christ Encounter, but then I realized that we would just have had, as Catholics, one intimate encounter with Christ in the mass, the Eucharist. Why not call it *Christ Encounter II*? The idea was that we would encounter Christ in each other as we pursued some kind of study. As that idea grew, I began to think of the encounter more broadly and came to the realization that the "curriculum" of the class was secondary to the experience of an encounter with Christ in our relationships. This idea blossomed into the realization that the community of faith was what we really wanted and needed. With that in mind, I formulated the first version of the proposal, which had the basic outline of much of this book. The proposal turned out to be seventeen pages long—single spaced. I am sure that scared the bejabbers out of them. *Who is this guy?*

The concept I was presenting was centered on a meeting after the 9:30 a.m. mass during the same time and in the same place as the parish held its "coffee and doughnuts" fellowship. In a parish the size of St. Mary's, there is no way that one community of faith can exist. What was needed was a way to break up a large congregation of over 2000 families into manageable units. The only logical choice for a manageable communal unit was the mass. Because of the number and timing of masses, it was impractical to try to have a group that the folks in all the masses could attend. With several masses each weekend, our best hope was to operate as if one of the masses was a potential community of faith. For Protestant churches, with multiple services, the "communal unit" might be the worship service. For smaller parishes, it might be the entire parish. Consequently, I decided to start the effort after the most highly attended mass. If it worked there, then we would consider trying to help start similar groups after the other masses.

At every turn, folks asked me what curriculum I would be using. I said that there would be no curriculum. We would, as a group, decide what we would like to study and forge ahead until we decided to study something else. In other words, the *content* of the gathering was secondary to the *process* that would unfold as we engaged each other in dialogue, prayer, play, etc.—essentially, we would be building a *community of faith.* While Scripture would be central to our learning focus, as Catholics, we would also be drawing on the *Catechism of the Catholic Church,* the documents of Vatican II, and the history of the Catholic Church. For Lutherans, focus might be on Scripture, the Catechisms of Luther, and the history of the Reformation. For Episcopalians, it could be Scripture, the *Book of Common Prayer,* and the development of Anglican theology. For Presbyterians, it could be Scripture, the *Institutes* of Calvin, and so forth. It was hoped that as members engaged each other in these learning discussions, trust would grow along with transparency—the fabric of the community of faith would gradually be woven together.

GETTING STARTED

After some changes of staff and a couple of years under my belt as a parishioner at St. Mary's, I finally got a hearing. The combination of my activity in the parish and the fact that the door-stop-sized proposal had been languishing for two years opened the door for serious consideration. The whole effort was approved on a trial basis in March of 2013. Some of us had already been meeting for several weeks before we got the go-ahead on Christ Encounter II. Jenny Diemunsch and I were co-leading this beachhead. We and others had chosen our first topic, Images of God, and had a list of scriptural passages that illustrated the many images of God in the Bible. We had about 5 people who wanted to continue under the new umbrella, so we started to call ourselves Christ Encounter II (CE2). The following is what the first handout looked like that we used at the Ministry Fair held on May 5, 2013:

Christ Encounter II

Building the Community of Faith

Every Sunday after 9:30 Mass
Marian Hall

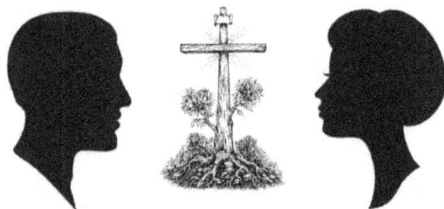

On the back was basic information regarding the scriptural source, mission, goal, model, and what I called the Twelve Pillars—which were the basic functions we would try to implement.

CHRIST ENCOUNTER II

Source: A new commandment I give to you, that you love one another; even as I have loved you, that you also love one another. By this all men will know that you are my disciples, if you have love for one another. (John 13: 34–35)

Mission: Building the community of faith by sharing with each other the love of Christ that we receive in our primary encounter with Christ, the Eucharist

Goal: To be transformed into the perfect likeness of Jesus Christ

Model: Ranger School for Christians

Weapons:
1. Holy Scripture
2. The Catechism of the Catholic Church
3. The Documents of Vatican II
4. The History of the Catholic Church

Motto: *Come and See!*

The Twelve Pillars:
1. To have a true and vital **experience** of the community of faith—to know our fellow Catholics as travelers on the same journey toward fullness in Christ.

2.   To **share** our journey with our fellow pilgrims that each may be lifted up and edified.

3.   To **learn** the profound truths found in the Catholic deposit of faith that point out the way, the truth, and the life associated with our lives in Christ.

4.   To engage in open and charitable **dialogue** that seeks only the truth of God and the consequent enlightenment of each member of the community.

5.   To **practice** living out our relationships toward others as we deepen our transformation into the likeness of Jesus Christ.

6.   To **pray** together as an expression of our vital relationship to Father, Son, Holy Spirit, and to each other.

7.   To learn to **play**—to engage each other with a lighthearted spirit of joy and delight that reflects a serious search for the truth without taking ourselves too seriously.

8.   To learn **accountability**—to learn to understand that each of us is important to the life of the others and that the actions of one influence the lives of all the others.

9.   To learn the pathway of **discernment** by learning to be open to the promptings of the Holy Spirit.

10.   To **minister** to others in times of need.

11.   To **evangelize** both within our own congregation and outside the Church so that others might participate in the rich and joy-filled experience of what it means to be a member of a Catholic community of faith.

12.   To search for opportunities and connections for meaningful **ecumenism**—the process of uniting the various expressions of the Christian faith in Jesus Christ.

Our first challenge was to expand participation. It was assumed that, while many mass attendees are "floaters" (they attend whichever mass is most convenient for them on any given weekend), there certainly was a core of folks who attended a given worship service regularly. It may be because they liked the music or it suited their weekend schedule better. As creatures of habit, we often will go to the same service because it fits into a particular rhythm on Sunday. Thus, any effort at community building should be designed to identify the core of a given service and within that core identify those who would be interested in helping to develop, lead, and "evangelize" a community of faith.

CE2 is not intended to be a small group experience. Like the early communities, CE2 will insist on the possibility that Christian community can be fed and nurtured in larger groups. If Jesus could have twelve apostles and many more disciples, we can learn to be in community with more than four or five. The NeoCats see the size of their communities as being from twenty to fifty members. Now that is more like it. Often we feel that larger groups are intimidating, if not to us, then to others. Jesus, as a model for our lives, was not the least bit intimidated by large groups. The man of love simply loved; the man of truth simply spoke the truth. The result was an implicit community of faith wherever he was present. If we take him as our model, there is no reason why we cannot learn to do the same.

In fact, the size of the round tables in the "fellowship hall" became an interesting logistic. The normal tables in Marian Hall, where we and about one hundred other folks had coffee and doughnuts after mass, were five feet in diameter and sat eight people. There were larger tables that were six feet in diameter and sat ten to twelve people. We managed to get one of the larger tables set up, and that determined our target group size. If we got a few more, we would scrunch together.

If we got many more, then we would split up into two tables. The trick here is to have a group that is big enough so that dialogue is lively and must necessarily include folks whose personalities might be a "challenge" for others (including myself). In other words, it is easy to love your pals. The community of faith is very different, with the objective of learning to love as Christ loved. If it were easy, everyone would be doing it. We really did not, however, know just how hard it would be.

What we found out very early was that holding a class with a curriculum is ridiculously easy compared to what we were trying to do. With a curriculum, people attend who are interested in the topic and expect the class to be stimulating. If it is stimulating, they stay. If it is not, they leave. In the open format of CE2, everyone is the teacher and everyone is the student. Folks need to be attracted to the *process* of building relationships that reflect the love of Christ without knowing what that actually is supposed to look like. It became clear that this was a leap of faith few were willing to take. Numbers fluctuated. Some came a couple of times and then disappeared—only to resurface and then disappear again. Others just drifted off. Many never gave us a look. It was clear that folks wanted something, but really did not know what it was they wanted or whether they had actually found it.

LEARNING AS WE GO

One thing was certain, we were learning as we went along. One discussion that cropped up concerned our meeting place. Since we were meeting toward the back of this large room, families liked to gather there with their children, and the kids loved to use our table as the "run-around." It was

pure pandemonium. Someone suggested that we might want
to meet in a quieter place. John Levine responded by saying
that our being here was a sign to others that they were welcome to join us. We all agreed—and stayed put.

We established some basic protocols: we would begin and
end with prayer (at least we try to do this), and we would
pray for anything else "at the drop of a hat." We usually had
to wait for folks to gather, because they wanted to connect
with their friends in a more social context before hunkering
down with Jesus, but once we got going we had some wonderful discussions. We decided to read an entire chapter instead of the few verses that were on our list.[107] We would read
the chapter and then open the discussion to anyone who had
a thought. No one did any research on the historical critical
context of the piece or its meaning. We just read it and responded. As a result we had little trouble relating the passage
to our own lives. This personal meaning seemed like a natural aspect of our deliberations. We would start after the end
of mass and mingling, which was about 11 a.m. and talk until
around noon. We found that we always had plenty of time
and everyone had an opportunity to offer their thoughts. We
eventually hit a point when we needed to move on in order
to "get through" the Scripture passages designated for that
day's discussion. Russell Chihoski piped up, "Do we have to
move on just for the sake of moving on?" *Hmmm, good question.* At that point, we agreed that we would take the time
we needed and not try to adhere to some artificial schedule. This decision singularly changed the whole tenor of our
discussions and the way they were guided. In other words,
there was much less need for the kind of facilitation that we

107 Eventually we turned to reading an entire book. The Baptists would
have been proud of us.

originally envisioned. We were tending toward what Scott Peck called "a group of all leaders."[108] Now, that is not entirely true, but certainly we were becoming a group where everyone felt empowered and could take ownership of the whole life of our little community.

Eventually Andrew Cober suggested that we needed to spend some time before our discussion of the day's topic sharing anything we would like to about our previous week. From then on we could no longer be confused with an ordinary discussion group. In other words, we were gradually adding more aspects of a fully developed community of faith.

One aspect of the meeting is worth noting. We always wanted the clergy to come and participate. Several times we had a member of the order of The Hearts of the Disciples of Jesus and Mary, Brother Philippe, attend. What was important was that he attended not as a leader, but as a participant. I think there is always a tendency for all of us to defer to the clergy, especially in matters of scriptural interpretation or Church doctrine. This is particularly true in the Catholic Church. What we believed from the start was that the clergy need a community of faith just as much as the rest of us. In fact, the Catholic clergy's status as sole leaders of the parish tends to make them somewhat isolated. While their participation has always been desired, it has gradually been offered more and more. Encouraging clergy of all denominations to *participate* in their respective communities of faith continues to be an important theme in CE2. We will keep trying to get them to come and join in, not so much as leaders, but as participants of the community of faith. It just so happens that they need us just as much as we need them. Recall our discussion of Jesus and his need for the apostles,

---

108 Peck, *The Different Drum*, 72–3.

as well as the apostles' profound need for him.

Having set the stage, it might be helpful to describe a couple of meetings. At one meeting, our Scripture passage was Jeremiah 18 and the image of God was that of the potter. We spent considerable time talking about the consistency of clay. If the clay is too watery, it cannot be formed. If the clay is too dry, it cannot be formed. We talked about how this works itself out in our own lives. No one had done any "class preparation" other than to read the passage. Insights came spontaneously from our communal deliberations. Because the format and the time frame were open-ended, there was space for the movement of the Holy Spirit. All we could do was to pray that this would happen, but we sensed we were on the right track.

A second meeting involved the discussion of the Book of Jonah. There were four of us and Jonah has four chapters, so we each read one chapter. We talked about the shade tree that God gave and then took away. We talked about God's judgment on the city of Nineveh and the fact that God withdrew his judgment once the people had repented of their ways. We then talked about how God dealt with Jonah and how God deals with us. We talked at length about the plant that God placed near Jonah to provide shade and comfort and how God does the same for us. But then there was the worm that killed the plant. The dialogue between God and Jonah about who is in charge was stunning. The story refused to take us to a comfortable place, and we struggled mightily with its meaning, but our time together was lively, insightful, and full of mutual interest and generosity. We were learning.

One of the most important revelations as we felt our way along was the importance of commitment. With the composition of the group constantly changing, the kind of familiarity and trust that we needed for open dialogue to develop was difficult to achieve. I found myself constantly wondering whether anyone would show up. I could always depend on seeing the smiling, generous, and receptive faces of a few stalwarts. Gradually, others started to see the worth of this kind of commitment, but to this day it continues to be a challenge to communicate the need for commitment while maintaining an open posture to new folks who need and want to *come and see.*

As far as the group dynamics is concerned, discussions are always lively and generate insights into the reading that seem to be edifying to all present. We never seem to wish that we had a curriculum to fall back on. The process of reading aloud a passage and discussing it seems to be just the right formula to lead us to a deeper sense of community.

THE FUTURE

Looking into the future, we really do not know if this will even work. It would be nice to be able to report that we were a raving success, but we are more concerned at this point with keeping our sanity, repeating often Paul's line, "I planted, Apollos watered, but God gave the growth" (1 Cor 3:6). We are merely planting and maybe watering, but we are totally dependent on God giving the increase. Our job is to be faithful—not successful.

In light of this humbling understanding, we also have a vision that someday we might teach other masses to do the same kind of community-building effort and might even be asked by other churches to show them how to do it. As we have struggled along, those visions have moved further and further off onto the horizon. A few things are clear, however: there will never be a curriculum, there will never be a limit on size, we will always invite the Holy Spirit to have a seat at the table, and we will always be plopped right in the center of any fellowship activity as a sign of the love of Christ active in the Christian community of faith. Pray for us!

25

FINAL THOUGHTS

This discussion of the Christian community of faith has been nothing short of inadequate. Each section of this discussion has proponents who are much better apologists than I. If there is any value in all of this, it may be mainly seen in the fact that a book like this exists at all. It may be similar to my opinion of Thomas à Kempis' *The Imitation of Christ*—the most important aspect of the book is the title. In the same vein, the most important aspect of this effort lies in its general agenda. There is no sense that the functions and characteristics of the Christian community of faith as stated here represent a closed universe of possibilities. They all overlap and are interrelated. The list undoubtedly is missing some important items that did not come to mind at this stage of my own development.

When I finished reading *Life Together* by Dietrich Bonhoeffer, I found myself questioning my own motives. He kept poking at me asking, "Whose agenda are you working on?" All I can say at this point is that I hope the driving force of all this is the deep desire to understand and experience the love of Christ and to offer an opportunity to share that love with others. The hope is that if Jesus were to walk into our parish, he would say, "I recognize these folks—even Jonathan—as my disciples."

Whether or not it is proper to talk of Jesus' admonition to us as the Eleventh Commandment is open to debate, but at least it is compelling. The call to love as Christ loved and to be recognized as his disciples by that love is central to our journeys as Christians. To the degree to which we all share that call, we also share in the desire that, through Christian communities of faith, the light of Christ may enlighten a world in need of healing and hope.

SELECT REFERENCES

Behe, Michael J. *Darwin's Black Box: The Biochemical Challenge to Evolution*. New York: Free Press, 2006.

Bonhoeffer, Dietrich. *Life Together*. New York: Harper & Row Publishers, 1954.

Casper, Walter. *The God of Jesus Christ*. New York: Continuum, 2012.

Claiborne, Shane. *The Irresistible Revolution*. Grand Rapids, MI: Zondervan, 2006.

Congar, Ives. *Diversity and Communion*. London: SCM Press Ltd, 1984.

De Lubac, Henri. *The Splendor of the Church*. San Francisco: Ignatius Press, 1999.

Doyle, Dennis M. *Communion Ecclesiology*. Maryknoll, NY: Orbis Books, 2000.

Dulles, Avery. *Models of the Church*. New York: Doubleday, 2002.

Fox, George. *The Journal of George Fox*. New York: Cosimo, 2007.

Grenz, Stanley J. *Theology for the Community of God.* Grand Rapids, MI: Eerdmans, 2000.

Kempis, Thomas à. *The Imitation of Christ.* London: Penguin Books, 1952.

Lewis, C. S. *Surprised by Joy* and *The Four Loves.* New York: Houghton Mifflin Harcourt, 2011.

Nisbet, Robert. *The Quest for Community.* Wilmington, DE: ISI Books, 1990.

Palmer, G. E. H., et. al., ed. *The Philokalia.* Winchester, MA: Faber and Faber, 1986.

Peck, Scott. *The Different Drum.* New York: Simon and Schuster, 1987.

Ratzinger, Joseph. *Introduction to Christianity.* New York: Seabury Press, 1969.

_____. *Called to Communion.* San Francisco: Ignatius Press, 1996.

_____. *Church, Ecumenism, and Politics.* San Francisco: Ignatius Press, 2008.

Rievaulx, Aelred of. *Spiritual Friendship.* Collegeville, MN: Liturgical Press, 2010.

Sine, Tom. *The New Conspirators.* Downers Grove IL: IVP Academic, 2008.

Snyder, Howard A. *The Community of the King*. Downers Grove, IL: IVP Academic, 2004.

Tillard, Jean-Marie. *Church of Churches: an Ecclesiology of Communion*. trans. R. G. DePeaux. Collegeville, MN: Liturgical Press, 1992.

Turner, Philip. *Sex, Money and Power*. Cambridge, MA: Cowley Publications, 1985.

Volf, Miroslav. *After our Likeness: The Church as the Image of the Trinity*. Grand Rapids, MI: Eerdmans, 1998.

White, Michael and Tom Corcoran. *Rebuilt*. Notre Dame, IN: Ave Maria Press, 2013.

Zizioulas, John D. *Being as Communion* (Crestwood, NY: St Vladimir's Seminary Press, 1997.

ACKNOWLEDGEMENTS

My first instinct is to thank all those in my life who have contributed to my meager understanding of love and community. My father, Robert Fletcher, taught me whatever I know about personal integrity. What you saw was what you got—and he did not have a disingenuous bone in his body. My mother, Gertrude Fletcher, unequivocally taught me what I know from experience as unconditional love. She might not have exhibited the kind of integrity that Dad offered precisely because her sole purpose was to operate with love in the best way she understood it. Because any community depends on both integrity and love, I would have to say that whatever foundation I have in each of these was laid by my father and mother.

One simply cannot press ahead with an agenda that is at odds with the status quo without support from others—those who periodically pick you up, dust you off, and shove you back into the fray. Father Gregory Carruthers, S.J., a professor at Saint Augustine's Seminary in Toronto, has been that force of continual support for me. I don't see how any of this could have taken shape without that encouragement.

Of course, my sister Penny, who was received into the Catholic Church the same time I was, has been a constant in my life since then—the one person with whom I speak practically on a daily basis, and who sees things from pretty much the same historical vantage point as I do. We have come from the same stock, had many of the same experiences, and value the same kinds of fruits that come from a life in the Spirit of God, although she is much further along that path in many ways than I am. She has been a deep resource of love, encouragement, insight, and support.

Mike DeVries is my editor. I write it and he offers some peripheral suggestions that may or may not help. Ha! That is a joke. I simply cannot say enough about my great fortune and blessing in being able to work with him on this project. Over and over again he offered knowledge and insight into many of the touchy points I was trying to make without the vast knowledge necessary to make them authoritatively. He repeatedly kept me from derailing and falling into traps that I was not prepared to deal with. When he would say that something I had said needed to be "nuanced" a bit more, what he was telling me was not to overshoot the bounds of my own knowledge—stay honest and stick to what you know. There is little of this work that has not benefited greatly from his knowledge and good sense. Every time I bounced up against one of his marginal comments (and there were many), I would groan, because I knew that I was going to have to deal with something that would be a challenge and require rethinking something. Once I had dealt with it, however, I knew that I and the book were better for the process. I cannot say enough about the debt I owe him. Any errors left behind are of my own making.

I would also like to thank Jarred Joplin for his design work on the cover and Caleb Seeling of Samizdat Creative for the layout of the text. Both of these men have been an integral part of my development as an author and publisher.

ABOUT THE AUTHOR

Jonathan Fletcher was born in Wilmington, Delaware in 1946—precisely nine months after his father was discharged from the U.S. Army Air Corps after World War II. His family, father Robert, mother Gertrude, and sister Penny, moved to Aiken, South Carolina in 1952 at the opening of the Savanah River Plant, an extension of the Manhattan Project designed to make plutonium for atomic bombs.

He attended both parochial and public schools, graduating from Aiken High School in 1964. He graduated from The University of the South (Sewanee) in 1968 with a B.A. in Chemistry. He received an M.S. in Geology from the University of South Carolina in 1972 and a PhD in Mineral Economics from the Pennsylvania State University in 1981.

He has worked as a management consultant, specializing in budgeting and planning, in a wide range of industries including oil and gas, maritime shipping, healthcare, and education.

He published his first book, *The Quiz: On the Nature of the Incarnation of Jesus Christ,* in 2012 and his second, *Human Drama Across the Curriculum: A Systems Educational Proposal,* later that same year. He resides in Littleton, Colorado.

www.ingramcontent.com/pod-product-compliance
Lightning Source LLC
Chambersburg PA
CBHW020149090426
42734CB00008B/757